Penrith Campus
Universit

T.

This ite
on o

BRITAIN'S ALPINE RIDGES

SNOWDONIA AND THE LAKE DISTRICT

Robin Ashcroft

First published in 1996 by
The Crowood Press Ltd
Ramsbury, Marlborough
Wiltshire SN8 2HR

This impression 1998

British Library Cataloguing-in-Publication Data

A catalogue record for this book is available from the British Library.

ISBN 1 85223 929 8

Dedication
This book is dedicated to my parents

Photo Credits

All photographs are by the author except as listed here: Jeremy Ashcroft,
routes 6, 28, 35, 36, 42 and 44; Ross Ashe-Creggan/AC Ventures, routes 1, 2 and 3;
Tony Shewell, routes 32, 39, 41 and front cover; and Graham Thompson, route 25.

Printed and bound by J. W. Arrowsmith Limited, Bristol

Rot

OCT 2

Contents

Preface

This book came about because for me – and I suspect for many other people – a knife-edged ridge or pinnacled arête has come to epitomize the classical alpine mountaineering route. Whether experienced in real life, or captured in a photograph, it remains a very potent image.

It is not difficult to understand why the early alpinists chose the ridge as the route for so many first ascents and why the ridge so often remains the 'normal route' to an alpine summit. First, it places the line of ascent above the worst effects of stonefall and avalanche. Secondly, while the situation on a crest is often exposed and exciting it does avoid unremitting steepness and is seldom too technically demanding or gymnastic.

Ascents via a mountain's other, more direct features – its open faces, buttresses, slabs, gullies or couloirs – tended to come after the summit was first gained and further, new challenges were needed to provide the impetus of a first ascent.

Perhaps this is a useful way to define the difference between mountaineering and climbing: a mountaineer is primarily interested in the summit and will choose the most obvious route to gain this, while a climber is more interested in overcoming a particular feature upon the mountain.

The generally accepted use of the word alpine can not really be applied to Britain's mountains. They do not have sufficient altitude or scale, they lack permanent snow cover and the glaciers have long since departed. Nevertheless, there are many places in our hills where a definite alpine atmosphere pervades. And a leap of imagination will do wonders to open up some fine expeditions.

Our peaks were, after all formed by the same action of thrust-folded terrain, glaciation and frost-thaw shattering. It just happened further back in the geological time scale. The alpine form still remains in our mountains, albeit on a slightly diminished level.

The routes in this book are listed because it was felt they had a character and atmosphere similar to that of an alpine ridge. The expeditions they provide are not as long or as demanding, but they certainly should not be underestimated.

Acknowledgements

Any guidebook inevitably draws upon previous works: the regional climbing guides of the Climbers Club and the Fell and Rock Climbing Club, for example, are marvellous references. Many early, and now lower-grade, rock climbs are often ignored by mainstream rock climbers, but provide great scope for scrambling and mountaineering.

The re-emergence of this type of route as a pursuit in its own right is largely due to the influence of Steve Ashton *(Scrambling in Snowdonia)* and Brian Evans *(Scrambles in the Lake District)*. The Bennet/Birkett/ Hyslop *Winter Climbs in the Lake District* and the Campbell/Newton *Welsh Winter Climbs* provide a year-round perspective.

More specifically, a number of people have directly assisted with, or had some influence upon, this book – often over a number of years and in some cases without being aware of it. I would now like to acknowledge and thank them all: Jeremy Ashcroft, Ross Ashe-Creggan/AC Ventures, Ian Atkins, Tim Barret, Tony Davidson, Towry Law, Andrew Longhurst, Pauline Moulam, Graham Thompson, David Varney and Daniel Westland.

In particular, I wish to thank Tony Shewell. Very special thanks, however, must go to Deborah and Olivia Scott-Ashcroft for their unstinting support, patience and understanding.

Introduction

The aim of this book is to identify and detail those ridges in Snowdonia and the Lake District that are 'alpine' in character and require a range of mountaineering skills for a successful ascent or traverse.

Many of these routes are traditionally referred to as scrambles, others should be described as rock climbs, a few – under typical conditions – can really only be regarded as rugged mountain walks, but are included because a covering of snow and ice transforms them into something much more challenging and altogether more spectacular. Perhaps a more comprehensive definition would be to refer to them all as mountaineering.

The criterion for including a route was that the ridge should have an alpine feel. In essence this means something with a narrow crest and steep drops on either side, or an arête that is perhaps blunter but has a significant drop below. In both cases under summer conditions the rock should be fairly continuous. An exception was made for some routes that in summer have little or no rock, but under full winter conditions accumulate snow and ice that forms a defined crest with sufficient exposure to make the use of ice axe and crampons mandatory.

It has to be acknowledged that snow and ice are very important factors in alpine mountaineering and that the British climate only generates snow cover for less than a third of the year. Nevertheless, it was felt that this could largely be discounted, for on many alpine ridges snow and ice are not a dominating factor once the glacier has been traversed and rock predominates on the ridge. Indeed there are far more rock routes in the Alps than purely snow and ice routes.

It should also be borne in mind that whilst the routes listed will probably only realize their full potential under winter conditions, they also then become a much more serious proposition. The routes can either lead to a summit or traverse a number of tops. Terrain of this nature is only found amongst Britain's high mountain ranges – Snowdonia, the Lake District and the Scottish Highlands.

USING THIS GUIDE

This book should be used in conjunction with the relevant Ordnance Survey map, both in planning and on the ground. The appropriate sheets are listed in the information block for each route. The 1:50,000 series gives good overall coverage, but the 1:25,000 series has additional detail necessary when travelling over the complex terrain that typifies most of these routes.

For sake of convenience the routes are set out by mountain ranges/fells. For Snowdonia they are listed in a south to north progression; for the Lake District they are listed by traditional fell groupings, but still follow a south to north progression.

Each route follows a standard layout:

Information Block

Mountain(s): Where the ridge/route is, and the height of the principal summit(s).

Category: Indicates the type of route, whether it is primarily a scramble, a full-blown mountaineering rock climb or a winter route. A route may be a combination of these categories or may be just one.

Grades: For scrambling, rock climbing and winter. Some routes will have more than one grade; for instance an upper-grade scramble may include sections of technical rock climbing. Most routes will be graded for winter; indeed, some routes will have only a winter grade as they have been listed because of their quality if snow and ice conditions prevail. See notes on grading and the grade table.

Time: The total time required – in good conditions and assuming a reasonable degree of fitness – to complete the approach, ascent/traverse of the route and the descent/return to the start point. It would probably take longer under full winter conditions.

Distance: The total distance of the complete expedition.

Height: The vertical height of the route, not including the approach.

Approach: A 6 figure grid reference and a brief description of the start of the most convenient approach and where it leaves the road.

Route: A 6 figure grid reference that pin-points the base/start of the route/traverse.

Maps: Appropriate Ordnance Survey sheet for both the 1:25,000 Outdoor Leisure and the 1:50,000 Landranger series.

Layout of Text

Introduction: A brief introduction to the route, highlighting its attractions and other points of interest.

Situation: Establishing the location, physical appearance and condition of the route. Directions will mainly be by compass point or occasionally left and right. Distances in kilometres and metres.

Ascent/traverse: An objective description of the route, its features and any problems likely to be encountered. Directions will be left and right and given as if facing the rock or in direction of travel. Distance/height in metres.

Descent: The most direct and safest return to the start point. Any scenic alternatives. Direction and distance as in approach.

Photographs and Diagrams

The purpose of the photographs accompanying the text is to be primarily informative, but hopefully also inspirational. In the first instance, when used with the diagram, they should give an indication of the course the route takes and idea of the type of terrain, difficulty and exposure involved. In the second, it is to be hoped that will convey something of the quality and grandeur of the route.

GRADING

This book uses the now well-established 4 stage (grades 1, 2, 3 and 3s) system for scrambling routes, the traditional method of grading rock climbs (Easy to Very Difficult), and the general winter/mixed climbing system (I–III) to grade the routes under winter conditions.

The book will use as far as possible those grades listed in the regional guides published by the Climbers Club and the Fell and Rock Climbing Club, plus established scrambling and winter guides. In the case of no established grade existing, then I have used my own judgement, employing well-known routes as a benchmark, but have tended towards caution.

It must be understood that any grade can only give a basic indication of the route and it normally applies to good conditions. In particular, considerable flexibility should be applied to the winter grades as a much more complex set of factors comes into play. A grade is no substitute for judgement once on the ground.

Scrambling Grades

Grade 1: This is a straightforward scramble, with little or no route-finding difficulty. The route can normally be varied or even avoided at will. Generally the exposure is not great, but even so, great care must be taken to avoid a slip.

Grade 2: This will contain longer and more difficult stretches of scrambling, where a rope may be found useful for safety in the exposed passages. Although individual sections of the route can usually be avoided, these sections may be inescapable once the scramble is under way.

Grade 3: This is a more serious proposition, only to be undertaken by competent parties. The use of a rope is advisable on the exposed sections or on the easy rock-climbing pitches. Good leadership is required, with the ability to judge how the rest of the party are coping with the situation and there should be no hesitation in employing the rope.

Grade 3s: This denotes a particularly serious route, perhaps containing very exposed passages on poor rock, which would be very serious for a solo mountaineer. A rope would normally be employed at some stage. Recommended only for experienced and competent mountaineers.

Rock Climbing Grades

In ascending order of difficulty:

Easy

Moderate

Difficult

Difficult (hard)

Very Difficult

Very Difficult (hard) to Extremely Severe: considered to be beyond the scope of this book.

Winter Grades

Grade I: Straightforward route, possibly on steep snow; risk of cornices.

Grade II: Route with short ice or mixed pitches.

Grade III: Serious climb having a much higher standard of difficulty with longer ice or mixed pitches.

Grade IV–VI Considered to be beyond the scope of this book.

Comparison of Grading Systems

The aim of this table is to give an overall comparison of the variety of grades that can be applied to the routes in this book. It can, however, only be regarded as a rough comparison.

Under typical conditions, many of the routes in this guide are hard to define and fall into a grey area. They vary from rough mountain walks with scrambling sections, through to established scrambles; some fall between scrambling and lower-grade rock climbs, while others are mountaineering rock climbs. This overlap can cause confusion and may even be dangerous, resulting in parties finding themselves in situations for which they are unprepared.

The problem becomes altogether more complex in winter. For instance, Cneifion Arête is listed in the Climbers Club Guide as a 'moderate' rock climb but is also regarded as a Grade 3s scramble. Under winter conditions it warrants a Grade III listing. If, however, you look at the definition of Winter Grade III, it is equated as being technically comparable with a Very Difficult rock climb!

The Environment

As mountaineers, one of the main reasons we go into the hills is to see and enjoy wild scenery; on this basis we should consider ourselves as its guardians. When compared with the

COMPARISON OF GRADING SYSTEMS

SCRAMBLING	ROCK CLIMBING	WINTER	BENCHMARK
GRADE 1	N/A	GRADE I	Sharp Edge or Pinnacle Ridge on Crib Goch
GRADE I	N/A	Mostly GRADE I/II, but possibly GRADE II	Tryfan's North Ridge or Bristly Ridge
GRADE 2	N/A	GRADE II	Dolmen Ridge
GRADE 3	EASY	GRADE II/III	Needle's Eye Arête
GRADE 3s	MODERATE	GRADE III	Cneifion Arête
GRADE 3s+	DIFFICULT	GRADE III and GRADE III+	First Pinnacle Rib
N/A	VERY DIFFICULT	GRADE III+	Needle Ridge
N/A	HARD V. DIFF– EXTREME GRADES	GRADE IV–VI+ N/A	N/A to routes in this book

long-standing activities of agriculture, industry and commerce, whose effects have had an impact on our mountains over hundreds of years, the impact of mountaineers is relatively small, but nonetheless significant.

It is vital that we consider our effect upon the enviroment at all times. It is easy to make sure we take our own rubbish with us, but what about picking up other people's? Dispose of bodily waste properly – carry a trowel! Stick to established and often reinforced paths to avoid further erosion if at all possible. Avoid disturbing birds, particularly their nests, and do not under any circumstances pick wild flowers.

Perhaps the most controversial factor affecting the environment is the car. Give some thought to using public transport or sharing vehicles with other parties, either from home, the youth hostel or the campsite.

ACCESS

Allied with the impact of recreational activities in the hills is the problem of access. Although every care has been taken in the preparation of this guide to utilize established rights of way, it can not be regarded as evidence of a 'Right of Way'. In the first instance look to the appropriate Ordnance Survey sheet, although the only fully up-to-date records are however the 'definitive maps' held by the county councils and National Park Authorities.

SAFETY

It is absolutely vital to understand that scrambling and mountaineering are not easier or safer alternatives to climbing. This pursuit will take you on to terrain where there is considerable exposure, without the all-embracing safety sys-

tems that are now commonly applied to technical rock climbing.

The adage 'a leader never falls' is no longer an essential demand placed upon the modern technical rock climber, it does however, remain essential for the scrambler and mountaineer. Although a fall is less likely on the type of ground described in this book, than it would be on an upper-grade rock climb; the consequence – if you were unroped – would probably be serious and possibly fatal.

The well-established methods of belaying a climb pitch by pitch are often too time consuming for the longer expeditions described here. Indeed the ability to move quickly but safely over exposed terrain is probably the most important safety element in alpine mountaineering. While it makes sense to fully belay a team on some of the more difficult pitches, it is also equally important to master the various techniques of moving roped together over the different types of terrain that will be encountered.

You should also be fully familiar with all types of abseil; not only the technique itself, but also the vital methods of anchoring and recovering the rope. While an abseil can quickly deliver you from a serious situation it is also potentially the most dangerous activity in mountaineering.

THE WINTER PERSPECTIVE

Broadly speaking, routes in the alps including ridges can be divided into three groups: primarily rock routes, snow and ice routes, and mixed routes (a combination of rock, snow and ice). This is over and above the glacier approach. On this basis, it is not therefore essential to have a covering of snow to make a route alpine in character, although it is fair to say that a sprinkling does much to enhance an alpine atmosphere.

Britain's mountains have snow for three to four months (if we are lucky), while alpine ranges have permanent snow cover, although this does vary on a seasonal basis. Most of the routes in this book can be done in either winter or normal conditions; a minority will need snow to bring them into an alpine category. The majority will be alpine throughout the year, but will be enhanced by snow and ice. Others – mostly the few technical rock climbs – will still be possible under winter conditions, but will probably appeal only to the mixed climbing expert who relishes steep rock, verglas and cold hands.

On the other hand, typical British winter conditions can not be equated directly with those of a typical alpine season, ie. the summer. They certainly will not be as warm. The classic alpine conditions of bright sun, blue skies and dry cold are a rarity in Britain. Typical winter weather is more likely to be high winds and wet/cold – probably the most dangerous type of weather a mountaineer can encounter. It can even be more severe, with truly Arctic conditions (this tends to apply to the Scottish Highlands rather than Snowdonia or the Lake District). There will certainly be less daylight.

The bulk of the routes in this book are traditionally defined as scrambling, this pursuit normally being regarded as a summer occupation. The same routes under winter conditions, however, will be altogether more serious, for instance that ever-popular and straightforward route Tryfan's North Ridge is given a winter grade II. A comparison between these routes and those in the Alps in the summer may require a leap of imagination, but in bad winter conditions they could prove to be more serious.

Personal organization and the experience to deal with the additional factors that prevail in winter – verglas, cornices, avalanche, gnawing cold, hypothermia and frostbite to name but a few – must be of a higher order. Additional techniques for the use of ice axe, crampons and snow belays must be practised. Accurate navigation is essential and a higher degree of fitness will be required. Clothing will need to be of a higher quality.

Three books are strongly recommended as a reference for all these techniques: *The Handbook of Climbing* by Alan Fyffe and Iain Peters (British Mountaineering Council) is both comprehensive and excellent; *Alpine Climbing* by John Barry (The Crowood Press) covers all aspect of alpine mountaineering; and *Scotland's Winter Mountain* by Martin Moran (David & Charles) has a very useful and concise chapter on all aspects of mountaineering on ridges.

EQUIPMENT

Weather conditions on Britain's mountains can be ferocious and the potential for accidents is always present. Having good quality mountain clothing is important. The best protection is provided by a 'layer' approach: an inner layer of synthetic underwear that wicks away sweat from the skin, a mid-layer of fibrepile that provides insulation, and an outer layer of breathable waterproof/windproof material. Good insulation must be provided for the hands and head as well.

You will need mountaineering rather than walking boots: a three-quater shank covers most contingencies in the summer, but a full shank is preferable for winter conditions. Do not neglect the quality of socks since they are essential for maintaining comfortable feet. Some form of gaiters are a help in the summer, and essential in winter.

In addition, belay gear (chockstones, slings and karabiners), a fully rated climbing harness, a rope (single 9mm is sufficient for the scrambling routes but an 11mm or double 9mm is needed for graded rock climbs), a helmet, and leather belay gloves (to prevent friction burns to hands in the event of having to hold a fall) will be required. In winter an ice axe, crampons and snow/ice belays (ice screws and, more usefully, a deadman) are essential.

A rucksack will be needed to carry all of this, a narrow profile sack with no side pockets and a minimum of straps being the best. External framed sacks are inappropriate.

In addition the following should always be carried in your rucksack:

Map of the relevant area and compass – make sure you know how to use them.
First Aid Kit.
Survival bag – man-size 500 gauge poly bag or Goretex.
Whistle – the international alpine distress signal is 6 blasts/flashes followed by a pause of one minute, then repeat. The response is 3 blasts/flashes.
Head torch.
Emergency rations.
Spare clothing – wrapped in a poly bag.

THE PERSONAL ELEMENT

The routes listed in this book cover a wide degree of difficulty and commitment. They vary from expeditions that fall well within a walker's itinerary, to full-blown – albeit lower-grade – mountaineering rock climbs. Winter conditions will make all the routes an altogether more serious proposition.

Never before in the history of mountaineering have so many well-equipped, well-read and well-instructed people been going into the hills. This is mostly all to the good, but sometimes it is achieved without serving a 'full apprenticeship' in the mountains. All too often parties come to grief by taking on something that on paper looks to be within their capability, the reality of changing conditions out on the ground puts them into situations which their experience has not as yet equipped them to deal with.

Risk is an integral part of mountaineering: everybody has to learn and this can only achieved by trying out something new and challenging. There is, however, something to be said for doing it in a gradual and progressive manner.

In the final analysis, the best of intentions and preparations count for nothing if you switch off and relax your concentration – this particularly applies in descent, which is when most accidents happen.

So please remember that mountains are dangerous places and are ventured on to at your own risk. Finally, this book is not an instruction manual and neither the author nor the publisher can accept any responsibility for any accident, injury, loss or damage on the routes listed here.

Snowdonia

Most of Wales can be regarded as hill country, but it is in the north, in Snowdonia, where the highest and most rugged mountains in Britain outside Scotland are to be found. A total of fourteen peaks rise to over 3,000ft (900m), including Yr Wyddfa (1,085m), Snowdon's summit and the highest peak in England and Wales. Of great interest to the mountaineer is the area's classic glaciated landscape of deep cirques (known locally as cwms), a large amount of naked rock and many fine sharp ridges.

Snowdonia's historical association with the early British alpine mountaineers was stronger than even the Lake District's. This is easy to understand as the peaks of Snowdonia have a more immediate alpine-like appearance when seen from the valley. The first ascents were done in the alpine context – climbing rock as a way of gaining a summit.

With the emergence of rock climbing's separate identity in the Lake District, Snowdonia's mountaineers quickly took to climbing for its own sake. Indeed the first domestic climbing club – the Climbers Club – was founded in 1898 and based upon the Snowdonian climbing fraternity.

The nature of Snowdonian terrain dictates that some skill on rock is needed to gain most summits. The distinction between mountain scrambling and mountain walking is often blurred. For instance, Crib Goch's Pinnacle Ridge, probably the most popular route in the district and one that is included in thousands of walkers' itineraries, is an exposed scramble in summer and a - full-blown mountaineering route under winter conditions. It is both illuminating and sobering to remember that this route has claimed the life of no less a person than a president of the Alpine Club!

Situation: All of the routes listed in this section lie within the Snowdonia National Park. The major mountain massifs tend to lie as extended ranges running roughly east to west and parallel to each other. They are all bounded by steep-sided valleys. In this guide they are listed in a south to north progression.

To the south of Snowdon, the ranges tend to be lower and consequently contain – in the context of this book – less terrain of interest. The notable exception is Cadair Idris. Off to the west, the Eifionydd Hills also have some rugged and mountainous terrain, as do the Moelwyns.

The next significant range is Snowdon itself. Its northern cwms contain several very fine routes, the most famous of which is Pinnacle Ridge on Crib Goch.

Next comes the Glyders, this range containing the highest proportion of good quality mountaineering and alpine ridge routes in Britain outside Scotland. To the north of the Ogwen Valley lies the final range, the Carneddau. Less dramatic than its neighbours, it nevertheless contains two fine ridges.

Snowdonia tends to receive less snow than the Lake District and much less than the Highlands. This is due to a more southerly situation and its proximity to the sea.

Approaches: Snowdonia is served by several major roads of which the A5 – which connects North Wales to the motorway network – is the most important. The main towns are Dolgellau, Betws-y-Coed and Llanberis, though they are remote from the base of the mountains. Youth hostels, campsites, B&Bs and numerous pubs are found in the valleys. Of particular interest are two centres based on what are now youth hostels; at Pen-Y-Pass at the summit of the Llanberis Pass, and Idwal Cottage in the Ogwen Valley. There is a rail connection to Betws-y-Coed.

Cadair Idris

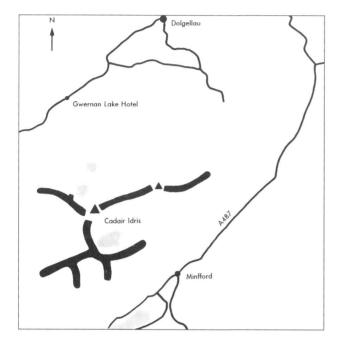

Route 1 – Cyfrwy Arête

Approaches: A470 from Blenau Ffestiniog or Dinas Mawddwy. Cadair Idris is signposted from Dolgellau. Bus to Dolgellau from Porthmadog, Blenau Ffestiniog, Welshpool, Bangor and Cardiff.

Accommodation: Camping – Ty Nant Bunkhouse and Kings YH; youth hostels – Kings (Dolgellau) and Corris; B&B and hotels – Dolgellau and Gwernan.

Tourist Information: Tel. 01341 422888.

Route 1

CYFRWY ARÊTE

Mountain: Cadair Idris (893m)

Category: Scrambling and winter route
Grades: Scrambling – 3s; climbing – Moderate; winter – II/III
Time: 5hrs
Distance: 10.4km
Height: 130m
Approach: GR 698 152; Ty-nant car park
Route: GR 705 136
Maps: OS 1:25000 Outdoor Leisure sheet 23; OS 1:50000 Landranger sheet 124

Introduction: Cyfrwy Arête has an important place in the history of mountaineering, for this was the first route attempted by Owen Glyn Jones, the man regarded by many as the father of modern rock climbing. It is easy to see why Jones was drawn to the arête, for it stands proud from Cadair Idris's great north wall and its steep line provides the ingredients for a classic mountaineering route.

Situation: A steep rock ridge formed by the cwm of Llyn y Gadair and the Cyfrwy face of Cadair Idris's northern wall. It rises from considerable scree slopes and is split into two: the lower section is a detached tower called Table Buttress, the upper part is the arête proper and consists of a steep pinnacled crest.

Approach: From the Ty-nant car park (the arête is obvious on a clear day) turn south west down the road, where after 100m you will reach a stile and tele-

phone box. Climb the stile and pick up the pony path as it winds through woodland. Above the tree line where a wall crosses the stream leave the pony path and head south east and follow a faint path that heads across the open hillside. Skirting below the Cyfrwy crags head for Llyn y Gadair. From a spot above the lake you will be able to cut up the scree to reach the base of Table Buttress.

Ascent: From the bottom you will be presented with rock that looks to be too steep. Off to the left lies a scree chute and a series of easily angled grass ledges that avoids the front of the buttress and provides access on to Table Buttress. The

Cyfrwy Arête

initials CA are scratched on a slab and they will definitely confirm your route finding. A steep arête should now be apparent above the marks; climb this on good holds until you reach a corner followed by a second arête which in turn provides access to The Table.

This is tilted at a noticeable angle and has to be crossed to reach a small col and the arête proper. From the col look left and find a short groove that provides access to an exposed arête; this should be ascended directly. Fortunately the holds are good although a rope should be employed from here upwards if it is not already in use. After 12m a move to the left leads to a small ledge followed by a corner that provides access to another section of the ridge.

The scrambling is now easier, although two small walls have to be overcome; they lead via a series of spikes, ledges, rock steps and a gully to the summit plateau and the top of the route.

Descent: The summit of Cadair Idris lies 1km to the east and is easily gained along a path that skirts the top of the crags that form its northern wall. From the top, the Foxes' Path descends steeply to Llyn y Gadair and back to the valley and the start point.

CA – Cyfrwy Arête;
T – The Table;
TB – Table Buttress;
ua – upper arête

19

The Eifionydd

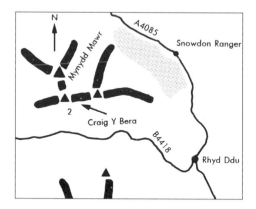

Route 2 – Sentries Ridge.

Approaches: A4085 and B4418 to Rhyd Ddu. Limited buses between Beddgelert and Caernarfon via Rhyd Ddu and Sherpa Bus service in summer.

Accommodation: Camping – Beddgelert and Betws Garmon; youth hostels – Snowdon Ranger; B&B and hotels – Beddgelert and Rhyd Ddu.

Tourist information: Tel. 01690 710665.

Route 2

SENTRIES RIDGE

Mountain: Mynydd Mawr (695m)
Category: Scrambling/climbing route
Grades: Scrambling – 3s; climbing – Moderate; winter – II
Time: 4–5hrs
Distance: 9.5km
Height: 150m
Approach: GR 568 539; there could be parking problems here, so an alterna-

tive start is at the designated car park near the Snowdon Ranger youth hostel, GR 565 551.
Route: GR 543 540
Maps: OS 1:25,000 Outdoor Leisure sheet 17; OS 1:50,000 Landranger sheet 115

Introduction: This route has links with the very early days of Welsh climbing. It was established by Archer Thomson, an early pioneer who greatly influenced the trend away from the claustrophobic confines of the 'gully era' of British climbing to the pursuit of bolder lines on open faces. He also wrote the first handy-sized practical climbing guide to the region.

This is a typical 'mountaineering rock climb' of that time. It follows a bold and direct line up a series of pinnacles that breach the Craig y Bera face of Mynydd Mawr. The high scrambling grade is, however, due more to the problems of loose rock than technical difficulty. It is nevertheless very exposed in places and you would be wise to protect yourself with a rope and running belays.

Situation: Mynydd Mawr lies to the south west of the Snowdon massif and receives much less attention than its neighbours to the north. Craig y Bera is found on its southern flank, which is quite unusual as most major rock faces have at least a partially northern or eastern orientation.

Craig Y Bera is nevertheless an impressive place, the face broken up into an interesting series of buttresses and steep arêtes. The centre of the crag is dominated by a massive set of pinnacles known as Central Buttress.

Sentries Ridge is to be found to the right of this, its base well up the scree slopes in the gully that forms the right hand boundary of Central Buttress. It effectively splits the upper reaches of this gully in two and it takes the form of a steep pinnacled arête.

Approach: Leave the road 100m to the south of the bridge where the A4085 crosses the Afon Gwyrfai and pick up the path that skirts the farm of Planwydd. Cross a stile and then walk towards the edge of a plantation where you will find a gate. A good path leads through the woodland in a westerly direction and emerges on to open hillside by another stile.

Turn right and walk in a north-westerly direction along the boundary of the plantation and climb towards the main ridge of Mynydd Mawr. At an obvious corner in the plantation perimeter (GR 553 543) leave the path and contour across the hillside on a fainter track.

Follow this, first across a scree slope, then to a wire fence complete with stile, followed by another scree slope, until the first buttress on Craig Y Bera is reached. Central Buttress is now very obvious and easy to identify by its notched crest; using this as a reference point, Sentries Ridge can be located. Go to the wide scree gully that borders Central Buttress on its right. Look up the gully and the slender arête in the centre is Sentries Ridge.

Ascent: The base of the ridge is only 6m above the track, avoid the first steep wall by climbing the scree slope to the right of the ridge. Access to the ridge proper is now possible and a climb of about 12m along the crest on loose rock

leads to a gap in the ridge. Above this is 30m of scrappy scrambling which comes to an end when the way is barred by an intimidating rock step. Traverse to the right and then ascend on good holds to regain the crest of the ridge.

Once back on the crest the fun really begins. Ahead lies a pinnacle followed by a knife-edge, leading in turn to a break in the ridge and then beyond a series of pinnacles. If the exposure proves too much there is a path which descends steeply to the right.

Turn the first pinnacle to either the left or the right; this move requires commitment as the holds are sloping, though fortunately the rock provides good friction. Beyond is the knife-edge, which stretches for 12m before it comes to an end at a gap with a rock slab on the far side. This should be taken directly and leads to another pronounced pinnacle. Scramble up for this for about 3m and then traverse right to a second notch and yet another, but smaller, pinnacle which is easily negotiated.

Beyond is a col which marks the end of the original route on Sentries Ridge; nevertheless, this is not the end of the scrambling and a series of ribs lead upward to the summit plateau of Mynydd Mawr. The route is disjointed and steep in places but a gully off to the right allows the difficulties to be avoided.

The end of the complete ridge is marked by three pronounced pinnacles: the first two are best avoided because of shattered rock and can be turned to the right; the third, however, can be taken directly. As you emerge on to the summit slopes look around to see a spectacular array of fantastically shaped pinnacles that dominate much of the face.

Descent: The path that follows the easterly ridge to the summit of Mynydd Mawr is close at hand, the top being

500m to the north, north west. To return to the start point follow this same path to the east until you pick up your outward path.

Sentries Ridge

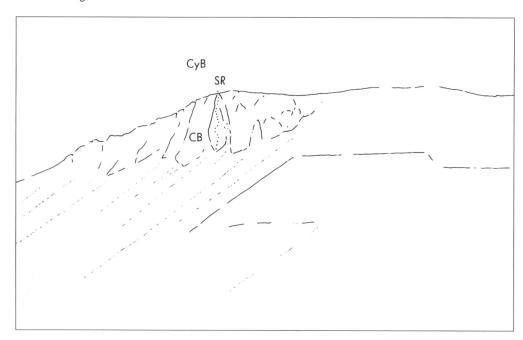

SR – Sentries Ridge; CYB – Craig Y Bera; CB – Central Buttress

The Moelwyns

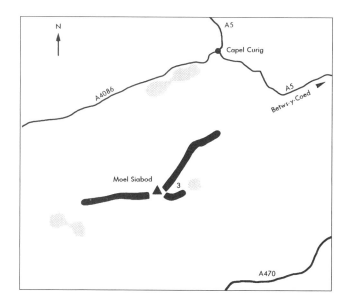

Route 3 – The Traverse of Moel Siabod

Approaches: A5 to Betws-Y-Coed and then on to Capel Curig. Rail and bus links to Betws-Y-Coed and Sherpa bus to Capel Curig.

Accommodation: Camping – Capel Curig; youth hostel – Capel Curig; B&B and hotels – Betws-Y-Coed and Capel Curig.

Tourist information: Tel. 01690 710665.

Route 3

THE TRAVERSE OF MOEL SIABOD

East and North-Eastern Ridges

Mountain: Moel Siabod (872m)
Category: Scrambling and winter route
Grades: Scrambling – 1; climbing – N/A; winter – I
Time: 4–5hrs
Distance: 8km
Height: 280m
Approach: GR 734 572; lay-by and bridge
Route: GR 713 546
Maps: OS 1:25,000 Outdoor Leisure sheet 16; OS 1:50,000 Landranger sheet 115

Introduction: The Moelwyns are known more for the quality of their hill walking and the ravages of quarrying than as a mountaineers' destination. They tend to be bypassed in preference for the major ranges a few kilometres to the west. While a traverse of Moel Siabod will never be regarded as a classic or technically demanding scramble it does make for a pleasant day on good rock. In winter conditions, it also makes for a fine but straightforward introduction to winter mountaineering.

Situation: Moel Siabod is at the north-eastern end of the Moelwyns, a dispersed and widely spread range that stretches to the south and east of Snowdon. It rises above the forest that clads the steep sides of the river valleys carved out by Afon Lledr and the Afon Llugwy as they converge on Betws-Y-Coed.

Moel Siabod takes the form of a whaleback, the north-east ridge being the major feature; the mountain has only one other ridge – its eastern ridge – which has the best scrambling. The south-eastern flank is the most rugged and holds the only cwm – contained by the aforementioned ridges – on the mountain. The east ridge consists of a broad but rocky and outcropped ridge broken by two significant rock steps as it rises steadily above Llyn y Foel. The north-eastern ridge is level and quite broad, but of continuous rock.

Approach: Leave the A5 by Pont Cyfyng and walk down the minor road to cross the spectacular Afon Lugwy gorge by the bridge. Take the second track off to the right as it climbs up the hillside through the woods. After 500m the track splits; take the right-hand branch toward the north-eastern ridge, which is now obvious. The track splits once again. This time take the left-hand branch to traverse below that ridge towards the eastern ridge.

Go to the north of what appears to be a lake, but is in fact a dammed reservoir and on to a flooded quarry which

Traverse of Moel Siabod

should be skirted to the south. The track ends at the quarry. A path continues over open hillside to Llyn y Foel. By now the rocky eastern ridge will be apparent as it rises above this fine cwm.

Ascent: From Llyn Y Foel climb the hillside and skirt round the end of the eastern ridge to its southern flank. A path can be seen ascending the ridge as it makes its way between, around and over small outcrops. There is no need to describe a defined route for the ridge can be ascended at will. At mid-height a broad shoulder emerges with a steady slope leading for 100m to the summit. The only difficulty comes in the form of an exposed slab, but even this presents few problems.

Descent: To the north east a broad and level ridge paved with rock slabs can be seen. Its traverse is straightforward, but each flank drops away steeply giving a marvellous feeling of space complete with fine views of Snowdon. After 1.5km the ridge drops steeply down grass to regain the open moorland and the outward path.

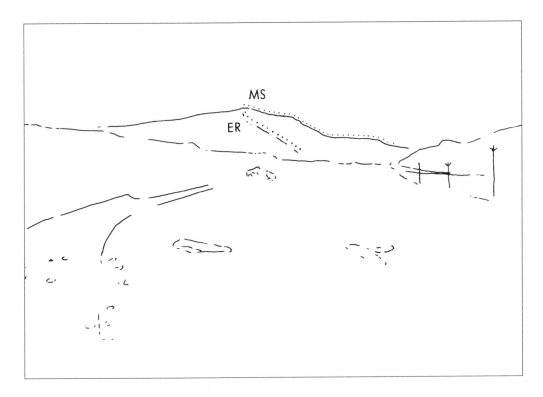

MS – Moel Siabod; ER – East Ridge.

Snowdon Massif

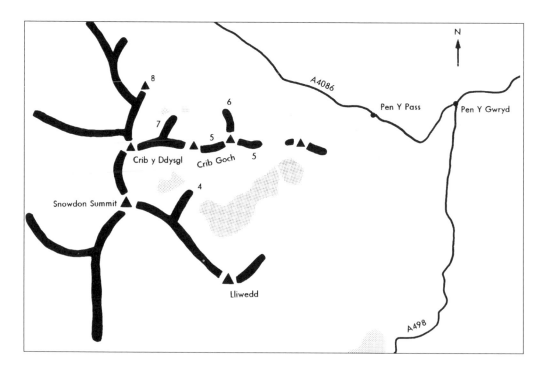

Route 4   – Cribau Ridge
Route 5   – The Classic Traverse of
              Crib Goch
Route 5a – Snowdon Horseshoe
Route 6   – Crib Goch's Northern Ridge
Route 7   – Clogwyn Y Person Arête
Route 8   – Gyrn Las Ridge

Approaches: A5 to Betws-y-Coed and Capel Curig, then A4086 to Pen Y Pass and the Llanberis Pass. Rail and bus link to Betws-y-Coed. Sherpa bus in summer to Pen Y Pass.

Accommodation: Camping – rough camping around Llanberis Pass; youth hostels – Pen Y Pass; B&B and hotels – Pen-Y-Gwryd, Llanberis and Capel Curig.

Tourist information: Tel. 01690 710665.

Route 4

CRIBAU RIDGE

Mountain: Snowdon (1,085m) – Lliwedd (898m)
Category: Scrambling and winter route
Grades: Scrambling – 1; climbing – N/A; winter – I
Time: 4–5hrs
Distance: 9.5km
Height: 200m
Approach: GR 647 556; Pen Y Pass car park
Route: GR 619 546
Map: OS 1:25,000 Outdoor Leisure sheet 17; OS 1:50,000 Landranger sheet 115

Introduction: Cribau Ridge or, to give it its anglicized name, The Gribin, is an ideal expedition for someone looking for a first mountaineering route to cut their teeth on. Even for its grade it is a straightforward scramble with no hidden difficulties or surprises. It nevertheless has many qualities that make for a classic ridge.

Its directness of line catches the eye. Once on the ridge you are committed to sticking to the route and there are no easier paths off to a flank. However, the rock is continuous, mostly firm with good friction and positive holds. It is exhilarating but never intimidating.

Situation: Cribau ridge rises above the waters of Glaslyn and its base is to be found just above the outflow of the lake. It is a spur jutting out from the Snowdon–Lliwedd ridge and is formed by the cwms of Glaslyn and Llyn Llydaw. When seen from the Llydaw side it tends to merge with the backdrop of Snowdon, but it can be easily seen by continuing past its base and viewing it from where the miners' track starts to climb above the lake. From here it can be viewed in clear profile as it rises in a continuous sweep to join the Snowdon Horseshoe.

Approach: The walk in could not be easier. Follow the winding Miners' Track up from the car park at Pen Y Pass, past Llyn Llydaw and on to the point where Afon Glaslyn flows out of the lake. Cross the stream as best you can and pick up the path that ascends the grassy knoll that forms the lower slope of the ridge.

Ascent: The grass soon gives way to some rough slabs of rock – even in the wet they provide sufficient friction – and it is a real pleasure to simply pad up them. Far too quickly, the ground falls away as you arrive atop a long plateau. The remainder of the ridge is seen soaring upwards some 170m away at the plateau's south-western end.

This is quickly reached and it shows that the strata of the rock rises from the lower right to the left as you face the ridge. There is no fixed route but one option is to ascend the ribs on the right-hand side, traversing round to the left as you ascend. The angle of ascent is sufficiently steep .o make the use of hands obligatory but the rock is firm and the holds obvious.

Eventually the angle eases when a quartz vein is reached, but after a short distance it steepens again for the final haul to the summit that is marked by an obvious cairn. The ground now opens out and you are on small plateau that forms the col between Snowdon to the north west and Lliwedd to the south-east.

Descent: Here you join the Snowdon Horseshoe at a point about two-thirds around the traverse. Following this well-known route in either direction is the best option for returning to the start, but an ascent of Lliwedd is probably the most attractive alternative. This is a fine ridge that just falls short of being included as a route in its own right.

There is, however, lots of rock and sufficient exposure to ensure an interesting scramble to the summit of this shapely and most alpine of peaks. From the summit of Lliwedd your route continues along the well-trodden final section of the Snowdon Horseshoe to join the Miners' Track by the causeway and then back to Pen Y Pass.

Cribau Ridge

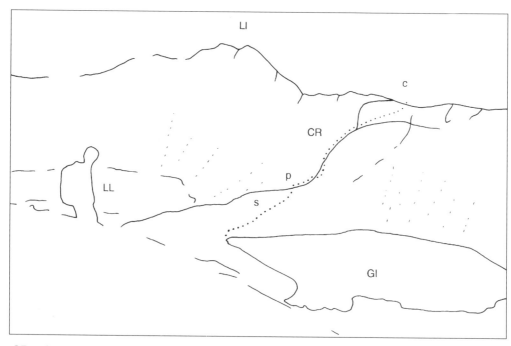

CR – Cribau Ridge; Ll – Lliwedd; LL – Llyn Llydaw; Gl – Glaslyn;
s – slabs; p – plateau; c – col

Route 5

THE CLASSIC TRAVERSE OF CRIB GOCH

Eastern and Pinnacle Ridges

Mountains: Crib Goch (923m) and Snowdon (1,085m)
Category: Scrambling and winter route
Grades: Scrambling – 1; climbing – N/A; winter – I/II
Time: 5hrs
Distance: 9km
Height: 300m
Approach: GR 647 556; Pen Y Pass
Route: GR 630 552
Maps: OS 1:25,000 Outdoor Leisure sheet 17; OS 1:50,000 Landranger sheet 115

Introduction: The traverse of Crib Goch by the Eastern and the Pinnacle Ridge is probably the best known and most popular expedition in Snowdonia. Typically undertaken as part of the Snowdon Horseshoe it is rightly regarded as a classic and has been a bridge between mountain walking and mountaineering for many people.

Despite its low grade it has a very definite alpine aura, as the view from its eastern summit will confirm. From here the ridge's razor edge and pinnacles have Snowdon's north face and eastern cwms as a backdrop and the situation is most definitely awe inspiring.

Situation: Crib Goch is a large spur that extends from the Snowdon massif towards the Llanberis Pass; to the north lies Cwm Uchaf, to the south Cwm Dyli. The mountain's level crest forms Pinnacle Ridge – a razor-edged crest with plunging flanks on both sides – and at its eastern end it terminates in a broad face bounded by two subsidiary ridges: the Eastern and the Northern Ridges.

Pinnacle Ridge is almost 500m in length and like the remainder of the mountain, consists of continuous rock. It can conveniently be split into two: the first two-thirds, a level knife-edge; and the final third, a series of three imposing pinnacles.

Sharing Crib Goch's eastern summit are both the Eastern and the Northern Ridges. Both provide good grade 1 ascents, but the Eastern Ridge is normally included in the classic traverse and the Snowdon Horseshoe. This rises above a col at Bwlch y Moch, its lower section consisting of a series of rock bands, the upper section a steadily ascending and quite airy arête.

The whole mountain can be seen to good effect from many viewpoints, but is hidden by Crib Goch's eastern flank from the start point and throughout the approach. It is not until the Eastern Ridge has been climbed and the subsidiary eastern summit reached that the ridge reveals itself.

Approach: From the car park seek out the Pyg track – it is well signposted. This provides a steady ascent for 1.5 km along a well-graded path; follow this to the col at Bwlch Y Moch. From here the path splits – the Pyg track descending west-south-west to traverse below Grib Goch; the ascent to Grib Goch leads due west and moves to steeper ground as the Eastern Ridge is approached.

Ascent/traverse: The going now becomes noticeably more difficult, but the path is obvious and cuts up scree slopes and broken crags until further advance is apparently stopped by a rock band. Polished footholds by a chimney indicate where the route breaks through the crags. After some awkward moves in the chimney a wider gully appears

29

and the angle eases as the upper section of the Eastern Ridge is gained. Running upwards at about 45 degrees, the rock is compact with lots of holds, hands are needed for balance rather than security. You can climb more or less at will, until the ridge starts to narrow below the summit.

At the top of the Eastern Ridge is Crib Goch's eastern and subsidiary summit, although it is often mistaken for the main summit, which is barely noticeable further down the ridge. From here the ridge reveals itself in all its glory and is by any definition an impressive site.

The way ahead is uncompromising but presents no major technical difficulties. The very confident will walk the crest, most will use it as a handhold relying on the footholds about 1m below. The edge is blunted in only a few places – one takes on the appearance of a small platform, the other is a very striking band of quartz that cuts straight through the rock.

Crib Goch's actual summit, marked on the map by a spot height (923m) is difficult to determine and is seldom recognized. Only 2m higher than the eastern top, a slight shift of gradient from ascent to descent is all there is to indicate its position. Beyond, after a further traverse down more knife-edged ridge, lie the three pinnacles, which are reached after descending to a small col.

Off to the left are signs of a path which weaves its way through the pin-

Classic Traverse of Crib Goch

nacles and traverses below their tops. To ascend each is an exposed business but presents little difficulty. The 6m scramble up the final pinnacle is the fitting finale to the route.

Descent: Beyond the pinnacles the nature of the ground alters drastically as you descend to a grassy col called Bwlch Coch. Ahead lie the summits of Crib Y Ddysgl and Snowdon itself – the path is well trodden, although very rough in places with sustained sections of excellent scrambling, particularly on Crib Y Ddysgl, which in places is of equal quality to the traverse on Crib Goch.

Should you want to return directly to Pen Y Pass, continue over Crib Y Ddysgl until the obvious standing stone that marks the top of the Pyg Miners Track is reached and descend that way. If not, then continue up to Snowdon summit and go along the Horseshoe.

It should be noted that under winter conditions there are some serious accident black spots on the descent route and that this is not a place to relax. Ice axe and crampons should continue to be used/worn. In particular the descent from the pinnacles to Bwlch Coch and the Crib Y Ddysgl ridge can ice over badly.

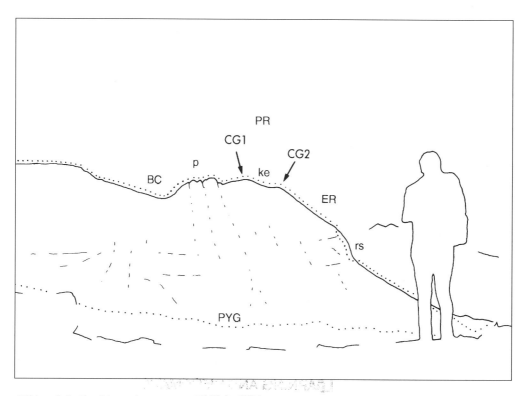

CG1 – Crib Goch's main summit; CG2 – Crib Goch's eastern (subsidiary) summit; ER – Eastern Ridge; PR – Pinnacle Ridge; BC – Bwlch Coch; PYG – Pyg Track; rs – rock step; ke – knife-edge; p – pinnacles

Route 5A

SNOWDON HORSESHOE

Mountain: Snowdon (1,085m)
Start/finish: GR 647 556; Pen Y Pass
Time: 7–9 hrs
Distance: 11km

Introduction: Although the traverse of Crib Goch and its pinnacles is the highlight of the Snowdon Horseshoe, the remainder of this traverse is a combination of superb lower-grade scrambling and rugged mountain walking. Such is its quality that it deserves inclusion here as the terrain is definitely alpine in character.

Route: After heading 150m south, to beyond the standing stone, the path joins the tracks of the Snowdon Mountain Railway and follows this to Yr Wyddfa (Snowdon Summit). The station is just below the summit which is reached by a very well-trodden path.

From the summit, descend steeply down the southern ridge for about 70m until the path splits; then head east to Bwlch Y Saethau and the top of Cribau (The Gribin). This section is a notorious accident black spot under winter conditions and ice axe and crampons should be used.

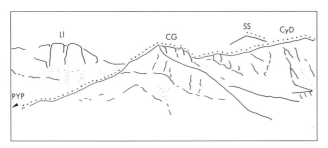

Snowdon Horseshoe: Pen Y Pass to Snowdon Summit
PYP – Pen Y Pass; CG – Crib Goch; CyD – Crib y Ddysgl;
SS – Snowdon Summit; Ll – Lliwedd

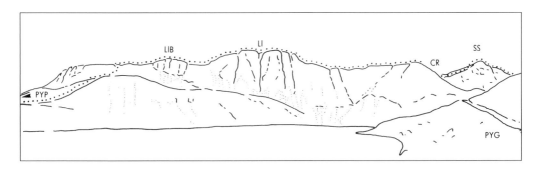

Snowdon Horseshoe: Snowdon: Summit to Lliwedd and on to Pen Y Pass
SS – Snowdon Summit; CR – Cribau Ridge; Ll – Lliwedd;
LlB – Lliwedd Bach; PYP – Pen Y Pass; PYG – Pyg Track

From here, Lliwedd's twin summits (818m) can be seen, its impressive northern face and western ridge must be one of the most distinct and impressive views in Snowdonia. Despite its alpine appearance this ridge falls just short of being a full-blown scramble, although sections of quite exposed scrambling can be found by sticking closely to the crest.

From Lliwedd's eastern summit, head to Lliwedd Bach, from where the path leads across scree slopes to Llyn Llydaw and the miners' track to Pen Y Pass. Assuming clear weather you will have had a good view of the full length of Crib Goch and Pinnacle Ridge.

Route 6

CRIB GOCH'S NORTHERN RIDGE

Mountain: Crib Goch (923m)
Category: Scrambling and winter route
Grades: Scrambling – 1; Climbing – N/A; winter – I
Time: 5hrs
Distance: 10km
Height: 290m
Approach: GR 647 556; Pen Y Pass
Route: GR 624 560
Maps: OS 1:25,000 Outdoor Leisure sheet 17; OS 1:50,000 Landranger sheet 115

Introduction: Crib Goch's Northern Ridge receives far less attention than the neighbouring Eastern Ridge. This is due more to its lack of convenience for inclusion in the Snowdon Horseshoe than any lack of intrinsic quality. But for the proximity of its more famous neighbour it would probably be regarded as one of Snowdonia's classic ridge scrambles.

It is a fine ridge, very much in the alpine mould with a sharp crest that maintains its edge for some distance and is continuous rock throughout. The situation is more remote and much quieter than the Eastern Ridge. In addition, its location is amongst the wild and spectacular terrain of Snowdon's north-western cwms.

Situation: Crib Goch is a large spur that extends from the Snowdon massif to the Llanberis Pass; to the north lies Cwm Uchaf, to the south Cwm Dyli. Its main crest is formed by the Pinnacle Ridge which is truncated at the Llanberis end by the mountain's rugged north-eastern flank and Cwm Beudy Mawr. The Northern Ridge is formed at the northern edge of the flank by Cwm Beudy Mawr and Cwm Uchaf to the west.

Crib Goch's Northern Ridge extends for over 500m; in its lower reaches it is quite broad, but it narrows to a well-defined edge as it approaches Crib Goch's eastern and subsidiary summit. The approach to the base of the ridge is

Crib Goch's Northern Ridge

barred by the impressive crag of Dinas Mot. The rock on either flank is often shattered but that on the crest – where the route lies – is surprisingly firm.

Approach: Leave Pen Y Pass by the Pyg Track and follow this for 1.4km towards the col at Bwlch Y Moch. Before the summit of the col leave the path and head north east to contour round Cwm Beudy Mawr. The path is vague but is marked by the occasional cairn; the going tends to be bog ridden. Stay above the steep rocks of Dinas Mot and continue around a grassy shoulder.

The lower sections of the ridge are broad and consist of grassy sections broken by rock slabs. A pronounced rock terrace extends from the base of the ridge and trends across the entrance of Cwm Glas Mawr. Gain the eastern end of the terrace.

Ascent: From the terrace cross some grass slopes broken by rock slabs. As the ridge ascends it starts to steepen and grass gives way to rock. A crest begins

to form, initially blocked by a steep rib of rock; this is climbed directly to gain the upper ridge which takes on the form of a classic knife-edged arête.

Stick to the crest to avoid loose rock and ascend the edge until it joins the Eastern Ridge just below the subsidiary eastern summit of Crib Goch. The going is very exposed but there are no major difficulties beyond the rib. Care, however, should be taken in full winter conditions as the rock is prone to verglas and in these conditions can be treacherous.

Descent: The Eastern Ridge is not recommended as a descent route because of the problems of reversing a rock step. Far better to continue on over Pinnacle Ridge, taking in Crib Goch's main summit and on to Crib Y Ddysgl (see Route 5: The Classic Traverse of Crib Goch). From here, if time is short, descend via the Pyg Track, or alternatively continue on over the Snowdon Horseshoe (see Route 5a: The Snowdon Horseshoe).

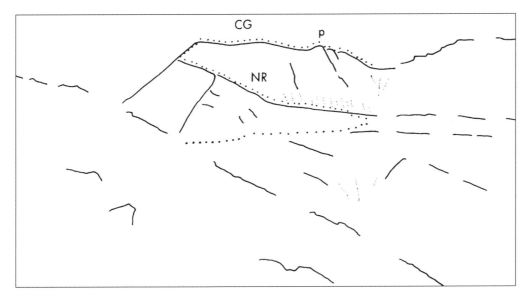

CG – Crib Goch; NR – Northern Ridge; p – pinnacles

Route 7

CLOGWYN Y PERSON ARÊTE

Mountains: Snowdon (1,085m) and Crib y Ddysgl (1,065m)
Category: Scrambling and winter route
Grades: Scrambling – 3; climbing – Moderate; winter – II/III
Time: 5–6hrs
Distance: 8km
Height: 250m
Approach: GR 623 570; bridge at Blaen-y-Nant
Route: GR 616 555
Maps: OS 1:25,000 Outdoor Leisure sheet 17; OS 1:50,000 Landranger sheet 115

Introduction: Snowdon's northern flank has some of the finest mountain terrain in Britain. Tucked away in Cwm Glas – one of her most solitary cwms – lies the Clogwyn Y Person Arête. This nose of solid rock provides a challenging scramble in very rugged surroundings and is one of the best scrambles in Snowdonia.

Situation: Cwm Glas is a hanging valley on two levels and its upper level is split in two by the Clogwyn Y Person Arête. To the north lies the Pass of Llanberis, to the south the Crib y Ddysgl ridge. Its close neighbour, Crib Goch, lies to the east and its spectacular pinnacles lend great atmosphere to the situation. The arête is shaped like an elongated Roman nose and is seen to

Clogwyn Y Person Arête

best effect from the pool called Llyn Bach. The compact rock of the ridge is broken only once by a large chimney that separates its tip from the rest of the feature and provides a gap in its defence.

Approach: Leave the road by a bridge that crosses the Afon Nant Peris 100m above its junction with the Afon Gennog. Once across this another smaller bridge will appear – use this to cross to the right bank of the Gennog. At first the path is difficult to see but if you follow the stream upwards a trail starts to emerge after 300m. After 1km the slope eases upon entering Cwm Glas Mawr.

The cwm appears to be blocked by an impressive headwall and seems to be a dead end. The route heads to the right and a faint line can be seen cutting through the scree and the slabs. After some scrambling up the slabs beside the waterfall a break in the skyline can be seen; this gives access to upper Cwm Glas. Continue to follow the stream and head for Llyn Bach.

Ascent: From Llyn Bach the arête and the chimney which provides access to the crest are easily identified. Once into the base of the gully a number of options are possible, but the most straightforward is up the large steps on the right wall of the cleft. The scrambling is steep but the holds are substantial and always present – after 25m the top of the gully, which is blocked by a jammed boulder, is gained.

The going now gets harder – it would

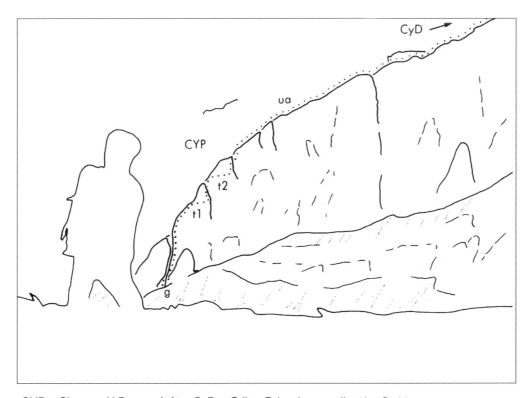

CYP – Clogwyn Y Person Arête; CyD – Crib y Ddysgl; g – gully; t1 – first terrace;
t2 – second terrace; ua – upper arête

be very awkward to reverse – and remains sustained for about 50m. Some awkward moves are required as the route traverses right, but again the holds are all substantial, obvious and on rough rock. Nevertheless there is a fair amount of exposure and it makes sense to use a rope – there are plenty of sound belays. Some easier ground on an obvious ledge then emerges.

Traverse to the right of the ledge – here a steep chimney breaks through the step and provides the way forward. The moves in the chimney are demanding and exposed, but as before comforting holds tend to appear in the right place – again a rope should be used.

The crux is now past and the going eases with some pleasant scrambling over smaller outcrops. As the ridge levels out, it also narrows, and this is a good place to relish the route and its situation. All too quickly this narrow section is crossed and the ridge starts to merge with the scree slopes of Crib y Ddysgl.

Descent: Having gained the main ridge of the Snowdon massif, a number of alternatives present themselves, including an ascent of Snowdon itself. The simplest descent to Pen Y Pass is by the Miners' or Pyg Track. Whilst being a useful fall back if the conditions deteriorate, it does involve a 3km roadwalk down the Llanberis Path to regain the start point.

Perhaps the best alternative – and one that will provide most interest as well as returning to the start point – is to traverse Crib Goch by the Pinnacle Ridge and then descend by its Northern Ridge to the lip of Cwm Uchaf. It is then a simple matter to descend into Cwm Glas Mor and pick up your original path back to the road.

Care, however, needs to be taken throughout this option, so make sure you have sufficient daylight and energy. The descent from Crib y Ddysgl can be challenging, particularly if covered in ice: this is a notorious black spot. The traverse of Crib Goch is equally uncompromising this way round, although you do get a much better view of the pinnacles. Finally, take care at the base of Crib Goch's Northern Ridge and do not stray on to the steep crags of Dinas Mot.

Route 8

GYRN LAS RIDGE

Mountain: Crib y Ddysgl (1,065m)
Category: Winter and scrambling route
Grades: Scrambling – 1; climbing – N/A; winter – I/II
Time: 6–7hrs
Distance: 6.5km
Height: 150m
Approach: GR 623 570; bridge at Blaen-y-Nant
Route: GR 614 563
Maps: OS 1:25,000 Outdoor Leisure sheet 17; OS 1:50,000 Landranger sheet 115

Introduction: The series of cwms that flank Snowdon's North-West Ridge contain some of the most complex and impressive mountain terrain in Britain. They rise directly and spectacularly above the north-west approach of the Llanberis Pass and are easily seen from the road. Less well known than the neighbouring Crib Goch ridges and the Clogwyn Y Person Arête, the Gyrn Las Ridge is regarded primarily as a winter climb, but is a fine expedition at any time of the year.

Situation: Gyrn Las is an extension of Crib y Ddysgl and Snowdon's North West Ridge. It is formed by Cwm Glas Bach and Cwm Hetau to the north west. The south-east flank is formed by Cwm Glas and Cwm Glas Mawr. Between the 650m and the 800m contour the ridge becomes steep, narrow and rocky. The lower ridge is truncated at the crag of Clogwyn Mawr and in its upper reaches it merges with Crib y Ddysgl.

Approach: Cross the Afon Nant Perris by the bridge and follow the track to the stile. Do not cross the stile, but turn to the north west and cross Afon Gennog by the bridge. Walk up the track, which gives way to an increasingly faint path that in turn gives way to open hillside. This does not, however, present a problem as the Gyrn Las Ridge has been in view for some time. Simply aim for the obvious shoulder; the going is steady and pleasant.

Ascent: The lower section of the ridge is fairly broad and at a relatively modest incline. There is no obvious route so a way must be made up, over and between the rock steps. At 600m the ridge steepens and narrows to a well-defined and narrow edge. Simply stick to the crest until the way is blocked by a series of steps. They can be avoided by some chimneys off to the right. After 150m the top of Gyrn Las is gained. The summit of Crib y Ddysgl is 750m to the south and is reached by following the ridge around the top of Cwm Glas.

Descent: At the top of Crib y Ddysgl, the Snowdon Horseshoe is gained and there are several alternatives for a descent route. All apart from the one described here will return you to the road some distance from the start point. This alternative not only returns to the start point but takes in a traverse of Crib Goch's Pinnacle Ridge and a descent by the Northern Ridge. This way the character and quality of the expedition is sustained right to the end. There are, however, some tricky sections on this descent so make sure there is sufficient daylight to complete it.

From the summit of Crib y Ddysgl, descend the crest of Garnedd Ugain to Bwlch Coch. The going here is quite difficult and deserves care – most specifically under winter condition or in poor visibility. This is a notorious accident black spot.

Particular care must be taken not to stray onto the upper section of Clogwyn Y Person Arête, which is easily done. This would lead to a horrendous descent with potentially dire consequences if you were unaware of your mistake. If in doubt take a compass bearing.

From Bwlch Coch, traverse the Pinnacles and gain the knife-edge of Grib Goch, then traverse to the eastern summit. Descend via the Northern Ridge taking care not to stray too far and on to the crags of Dinas Mot. From the shoulder at the bottom of the ridge traverse into Cwm Glas Mawr and pick up the faint path that returns to the valley.

Gyrn Las Ridge

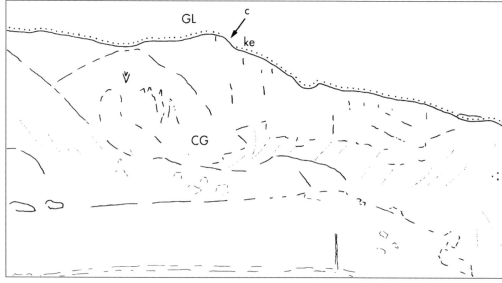

GL – Gyrn Las; CG – Cwm Glas; ke – knife-edge; c – chimney

The Glyders

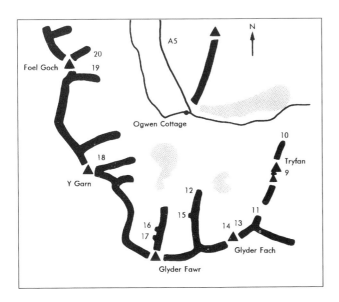

Route 9   – First Pinnacle Rib
Route 10   – Tryfan's North Ridge
Route 11   – Bristly Ridge
Route 12   – Gribin Ridge
Route 12a – Tryfan–Glyder Traverse
Route 13   – East Gully Arête
Route 14   – Dolmen Ridge
Route 15   – Cneifion Arête
Route 16   – East Arête of Glyder Fawr
Route 17   – Central Arête of Glyder
              Fawr
Route 18   – Traverse of Y Garn
Route 19   – Needle's Eye Arête
Route 20   – Yr Esgair

Approaches: A5 to Betws-Y-Coed and Bethesda. Rail and bus link to Betws-Y-Coed. Limited bus service to Ogwen Cottage. Sherpa bus service in summer.

Accommodation: Camping – established sites in Ogwen Valley; youth hostels – Idwal Cottage (at Ogwen Cottage);

B&B and hotels – Pen-Y-Gwryd, Capel Curig and Bethesda.

Tourist information: Tel. 01690 710665.

Route 9

FIRST PINNACLE RIB

Mountain: Tryfan (915m)
Category: Rock climb
Grades: Scrambling – N/A; climbing – Difficult; winter – N/A
Time: 6–8hrs
Distance: 2.5km
Height: 170m
Approach: GR 668 605; opposite Glan Dana
Route: GR 665 593
Maps: OS 1:25,000 Outdoor Leisure sheet 17; 1:50,000 Landranger sheet 115

Introduction: Tryfan and its North

Ridge has a well-established reputation as a route that marks a transition from mountain walking to scrambling and/or mountaineering. The mountain's East Face has an equally high reputation as a fertile ground for mountaineering rock climbs.

First Pinnacle Rib is a classic example of the latter, and follows a well-defined arête from the Heather Terrace directly to the summit. Although of a modest grade, much of the climbing is quite delicate and often exposed; an unprotected fall would be serious and possibly fatal. In addition, the route has the odd surprise. *It is essential that the route is climbed using fixed belays and that the pitches are fully protected with running belays.*

Situation: Tryfan's North Ridge, the

East Face and the rising traverse of the Heather Terrace are obvious landmarks for anyone familiar with the Ogwen Valley. The three buttresses and their associated summits also stand out and are easily recognized. The middle buttress – known as Central Buttress – forms Tryfan's rocky summit.

Central Buttress is defined to the south by South Gully and to the north by North Gully. First Pinnacle Rib rises just to the north of South Gully and follows the crest of a broad arête to a pinnacle – after which the route is named – before merging into less well-defined ground just below the summit.

Approach: Leave the A5 opposite Glan Dana by the stile and follow the track east towards Gwern Gof Uchaf. Before the farm turn south west below Tryfan

First Pinnacle Rib

Bach (Little Tryfan) and then ascend with increasing steepness the narrow path that winds up the initial slopes of Tryfan's North Ridge to gain the northern end of the Heather Terrace. Be careful to avoid the subsidiary terrace that lies below the Heather Terrace.

Once on the Heather Terrace, follow this as it traverses across Tryfan's East Face. Locating the Central Buttress can be confusing, but an obvious split block marks Little Gully which is a feature on the northern side of Central Buttress. After the block is a large bay, which lies just to the north of South Gully. South Gully is the best reference for locating First Pinnacle Rib.

Ascent: The start of First Pinnacle Rib lies 10m to the right of the northern edge of South Gully. The first pitch climbs a slab that ascends underneath and to the right of a pronounced bulge at the base of the arête. After about 7m, you can then move to the left to gain a crack system that provides access to the broad crest of the ridge.

The ridge is an airy and exciting place. The climbing is mostly straightforward, tending to be delicate rather than strenuous. The key is to look for the holds and to trust to the superb rock. Protection is apparent and plentiful so the placement of running belays is straightforward. At least two pitches will be needed.

After 80m the ridge comes to an end and this is marked by a very obvious pinnacle. Behind the pinnacle is the sting in the tail. Ahead is a compact, rippled and steep slab. This is Yellow Slab and the test piece of the route. The

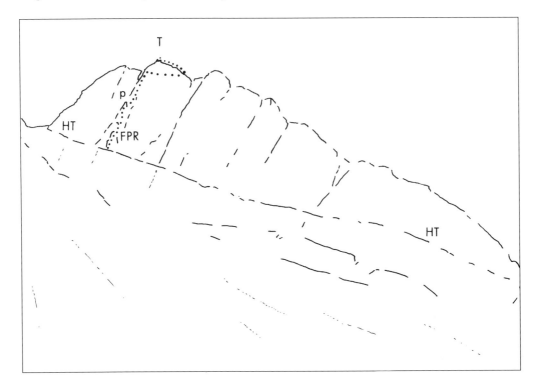

T – Tryfan (summit); FPR – First Pinnacle Rib; HT – Heather Terrace; p – pinnacle

one line of weakness is a crack some 2.5m above the ledge. This is gained by some very delicate friction moves after which the going eases.

It should, however, be stressed that although the overall grade of the route is only 'Difficult', this series of moves is closer to 'Very Severe'. The moves are also almost impossible if the rock is wet or iced up.

If you do not aspire to being a VS climber or the weather prohibits the slab, move right, around a bulge, to ascend on easier ground up a crack and a wall before moving back left above Yellow Slab to a ledge. The ridge is now regained and ascended directly via a curving groove. The going is steep and the quality of the rock deteriorates as height is gained, so continue to take care and fully protect yourself with rope and belays.

After 45m the ridge starts to merge with the mountain and eventually disappears below the summit headwall. Two options exist here. The most straightforward is to traverse to the right on ledges to gain the North Ridge and straightforward access to the sum-mit. If you are fired up and want more punishment, then look to the left and Thompson's Chimney. It does, however, have to be said that this is a very strenuous, 'Very Difficult' climb and well outside the remit of this book.

Descent: From the summit of Tryfan there are several descent options. The most direct is to descend via the North Ridge, but this is only feasible if you have experience of the route in ascent. If in doubt, descend by either the Western Gully or down the South Ridge.

If you opt for the North Ridge seek out a path that lies below the crest of the ridge on the eastern side. This can be reached from the top down a series of slabs to the east of the summit area.

For the Western Gully: from the summit go north and then almost immediately west down the scree. The path is well worn and obvious and quickly gains the gentler lower slopes and then the road. The South Ridge is the most popular route on Tryfan and is cairned. It leads to Bwich Tryfan and then to the Cwm Bochlwyd path.

Route 10

TRYFAN'S NORTH RIDGE

Mountain: Tryfan (913m)
Category: Scrambling and winter route
Grades: Scrambling – 1; climbing – N/A; winter – I/II
Time: 4–5hrs
Distance: 2.6km
Height: 520m
Approach: GR:663 602 – lay-bys on A5
Route: GR 663 601
Map: OS 1:25,000 Outdoor Leisure sheet 17; 1:50,000 Landranger sheet 115

Introduction: One of the most exciting sights in Snowdonia must be the first glimpse of Tryfan as the A5 enters the Ogwen Valley. This shark's fin of a mountain is girdled by rock on all sides and stands in isolated splendour. A mountaineer's eye will be irresistibly drawn to the North Ridge, the ascent of which is an adventurous expedition that is completely alpine in character.

Situation: Tryfan is an isolated outlier of the Glyder range connected only by the narrow col of Bwlch Tryfan. It takes the form of an elongated rock ridge, with both flanks buttressed by steep cliffs. There are no 'walking only' ways to the summit and Tryfan is the only mountain in England and Wales where hands must be used at some stage on any route to gain the summit.

The Northern Ridge rises dramatically in a single sweep from valley floor to rocky summit. A broad arête rather than a knife-edged crest, the rock is sound with plenty of good holds and the sense of exposure is seldom too intimidating.

Approach: The walk in is both brutal and thankfully short. Leave the A5 where a stile crosses the wall near the lay-bys. The path is well worn and ascends steeply below and to the left of the Milestone Buttress. A series of small gullies provides a break through the small crags that flank the ridge's lower slope. After about 100m of steep and scrappy scrambling the crest line is reached.

Ascent: A plateau of quartzite-covered rock indicates that you have gained the main crest of the ridge and this is a good place to view the route. Although the ridge is not of the knife-edge variety, the mountain architecture is impressive. Off to the right the route is of continuous rock and the main crest – where the best scrambling is found – becomes apparent as you ascend.

After a short distance a pronounced rock called The Cannon – apparently ranged on the road below – is reached; beyond lies the most serious section. Move initially to the left to avoid steep rock, but then return to the right. From here the crest remains narrow and the going is exposed.

This section is brought to an end by a small col formed by the top of Nor' Nor' Gully. From here there is a series of rock steps and subsidiary tops and although there are short sections of steep scrambling the overall angle of the ridge starts to ease. Eventually the crest merges into a gully system below the northern summit.

Continue up and over this up to the top – the final summit is unmistakable as the ground falls away in all directions. The actual peak is marked by two small gendarmes – called Adam and Eve. It is a traditional trick to leap between these, but care should be taken as a slip could be disastrous.

Descent: From the summit, descend the

South Ridge; while some scrambling is required at mid-height the going is a lot easier than the previous ascent. The path is obvious at first, but it does become vague as it breaks through a series of steps. There are, however, some strategically placed cairns that indicate the way ahead. This will lead to the col at Bwlch Tryfan from where the miners' track can be followed to Llyn Bochlwyd from where several paths lead to the road.

Tryfan's North Ridge

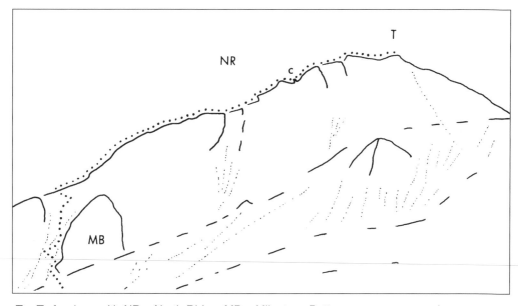

T – Tryfan (summit); NR – North Ridge; MB – Milestone Buttress; c – cannon rock

Route 11

BRISTLY RIDGE

Mountain: Glyder Fach (994m)
Category: Scrambling and winter route
Grades: Scrambling – 1; climbing –
N/A; winter – II
Time: 4hrs
Distance: 5.2km
Height: 140m
Approach: GR 650 603; Ogwen Cottage
Route: GR 661 588
Maps: OS 1:25,000 Outdoor Leisure
Sheet 17; OS 1:50,000 Landranger sheet
115

Introduction: Bristly Ridge presents a
steep and intimidating prospect as it
climbs upward in a continuous line from
the col at Bwlch Tryfan. Only a grade 1
scramble, it should still be treated with
respect for its pinnacled crest is exposed
and requires boldness during an ascent.
The rock is sound, the holds are obvious
and it provides both an adventurous
and satisfyingly direct route to the summit plateau of the Glyders.

Situation: A steep rock ridge that juts
out from the Glyder massif and connects outlying Tryfan with the main
range. Bordered by the steep scree
slopes and headwall of Cwm Tryfan on
its east flank and Cwm Bochlwyd to the
west, it presents a jagged profile with
several pronounced pinnacles and gaps
on its upper reaches. When seen head
on, it has a sufficiently pronounced line
to make it stand out from the surrounding crags and it can be seen to narrow in
its upper reaches.

Approach: From Ogwen Cottage head
directly by the obvious path to the outflow from Llyn Bochlwyd. Skirt around
the east side of the lake and follow the
path to Bwlch Tryfan, which is the col
between Tryfan's south ridge and the
Glyder massif. At the crest of this pass is
a dry stone wall; turn south west and
follow the wall until it comes to an end
– this is the base of Bristly Ridge.

Ascent: Beyond the wall can be seen a
small curved scree slope trending to the
right and topped by a gully. Go into the
gully and climb it via a series of easy
ledges; the gully is blocked by a chockstone after 18m of climbing, but this can
easily be bypassed. The gully narrows
to an obvious groove topped by a series
of pinnacles. This provides access to a
shoulder on the main crest of the ridge.

Follow the polished rock along the
ridge; initially you will be forced right
to cross an angled slab before regaining
the main crest. On the crest the going
becomes steeper, but eventually the first
of a series of pinnacles emerges. This is
traversed to the left before dropping
down into a deep gap.

The next pinnacle is traversed to the
right and then into a gully before yet
another one appears, which is traversed
to the left. From a gap at it its base,
known as Great Pinnacle Gap, the final
pinnacle appears. This can easily be
ascended on either side to a gangway
from where the whole ridge can be seen
falling away below your feet.

The angle now eases and the route
lies among a series of smaller pinnacles
that mark the top of the ridge. The
ground falls away as you emerge on to
the open plateau of the Glyders.

Descent: From here the fastest descent
is to head east-south-east along the path
that skirts to the top of the crags that
form the headwall of Cwm Tryfan for
750m until the Miners' Track is reached.
Follow this back to Bwlch Tryfan and
then return by your original route.

Bristly Ridge

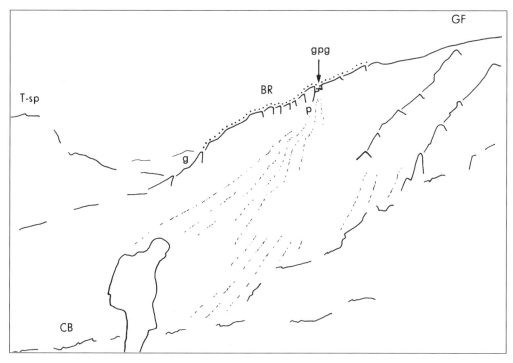

BR – Bristly Ridge; GF – Glyder Fach; CB – Cwm Bochlwyd; T-sp – Tryfan's south peak;
g – gully; p – pinnacles; gpg – great pinnacle gap

Route 12

GRIBIN RIDGE

Mountains: Glyder Fach (994m) and Glyder Fawr (999m)
Category: Scrambling and winter route
Grades: Scrambling – 1; climbing – N/A; winter – I/II
Time: 4–5 hrs
Distance: 7.5km
Height: 150m
Approach: GR 650 603; Ogwen Cottage
Route: GR 651 587
Maps: OS 1:25,000 Outdoor Leisure sheet 17; OS 1:50,000 Landranger sheet 115

Introduction: Gribin Ridge provides a direct, interesting and relatively straightforward way of gaining the Glyder plateau from the Ogwen Valley. Its surroundings are impressive and it is easy to understand why it is such a popular route. Most of the way, it is a simple stroll along a broad but airy ridge, only becoming a scramble in the final section .Here the crest steepens dramatically into a narrow rocky arête which has a pronounced sense of exposure.

The long and easy section of the ridge can be avoided for something more adventurous by using a broken buttress that rises from Cwm Bochlwyd, instead of following all of the ridge along the traditional route.

Situation: Gribin Ridge falls away from the Glyder plateau between the summits of Glyder Fach and Glyder Fawr and the lower ridge is truncated at the Gribin Facet. To the east, overlooked by steep slopes, lies Cwm Bochlwyd; to the west, Cwm Cneifion and Cwm Idwal.

The lower part is a broad rocky ridge that eventually leads on to a plateau. The eastern edge of this plateau is marked by a craggy edge, and it is from this that the scrambling section rises as the ridge narrows and then steepens to about 45 degrees, 100m below the edge of the Glyders. It is marked on the OS map as Y Gribin and should not be confused with Cribau Ridge on Snowdon, which is often anglicized to 'The Gribin'.

Approach: From the car parks at Ogwen Cottage, pick up the well-worn path that heads south east and then south west to the outflow of Llyn Idwal. Follow the eastern shore of the lake for 230m until the rocks of the Gribin Facet are cleared. Ascend up the path that follows the small stream to the bluff above the facet.

After about 180m of ascent and 750m in distance, the crest of the lower Gribin Ridge is reached. A path heads south between small crags: follow this for 700m until an obvious plateau is gained. The upper section of the ridge is now apparent as the crest rises from the crest of the eastern edge of the plateau.

Alternative approach: A subsidiary spur rises from Cwm Bochlwyd to join the eastern flank of Gribin Ridge. It is a more direct and continuous ascent, making for an adventurous expedition.

From Ogwen Cottage head south west along the obvious track to Llyn Bochlwyd and then skirt around the western shore of the lake. An obvious spur can be seen ascending to join the eastern side of Gribin Ridge. This narrows as it climbs and can be ascended over broken but continuous rock. This leads to the plateau on the main ridge. The crest of the upper section of Gribin Ridge appears to be a direct continuation of this, rather than the main ridge.

Ascent: From the plateau, move to the

Gribin Ridge

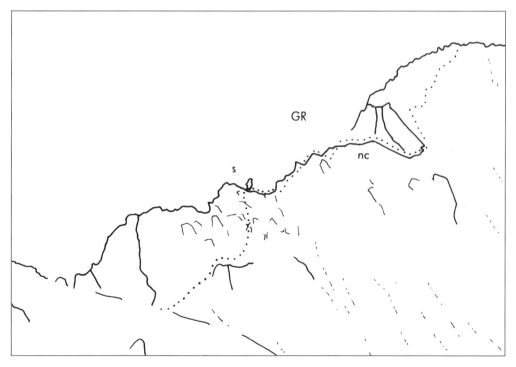

GR – Gribin Ridge; s – slabs; nc – narrow crest

well-defined crest and ignore the path off to the right-hand side. The first section consists of easily angled rock slabs that provide some quite delicate moves on good holds. The crest now levels and narrows and a series of small pinnacles must be negotiated. This stretch provides a real sense of exposure for the left flank falls away steeply.

Once this is cleared the ridge steepens again as it starts to join the main massif of the Glyders and the crest broadens into a buttress. The route then ascends via a series of small gullies until the ground falls away and the summit plateau emerges.

Descent: The ridge does not lead directly to a summit but emerges between Glyder Fach and Glyder Fawr, both of which are within easy walking distance.

The Glyders are a mysterious and fascinating place. They consist of a wide plateau dotted with frost-shattered peaks, the most interesting of which are the Castle of the Winds and the famous Cantilever Rock.

The most direct way back to Ogwen Cottage is by returning down Gribin Ridge, which is relatively straightforward if the path on the western flank is used (see Route 12a Tryfan–Glyder Traverse). There are, however, several attractive alternatives including a traverse of the Glyders to Y Garn (947m) and a descent via the North East Ridge.

A particularly spectacular alternative is to drop down via Llyn y Cwm and get on to the path that goes down beside the great chasm of the Devils Kitchen, the Idwal Slabs and on to Llyn Idwal, then pick up the outward path.

Route 12A

TRYFAN–GLYDER TRAVERSE

Mountains: Tryfan (915m) and Glyder Fach (994m)
Time: 7–8hrs
Distance: 6km
Height: 1,223m
Start: GR 663 602; lay-bys on A5
Descent: GR 651 582; top of Gribin Ridge
Finish: GR 650 603; Ogwen Cottage

Introduction: This traverse links together the three previous routes. It involves a traverse of Tryfan by the North and South Ridges, then an ascent to the Glyder Plateau by Bristly Ridge and a descent via Gribin Ridge.

Much of the traverse is spent on ground that fits the alpine form; it is mostly straightforward but offers superb scrambling. It makes for a long and demanding day; for all but the stronger parties it would be impractical in winter.

Route: This expedition follows Tryfan's North and South Ridge and Bristly Ridge as outlined in Routes 10 and 11, but then reverses Route 12 – Gribin Ridge.

To gain Gribin Ridge follow the path heading south-west from the summit of Glyder Fach towards Castell Y Gwynt and around the top of Cwm Bochlwyd to a split in the path, then follow the branch that heads north west and you will reach Gribin Ridge about 200m from the junction.

Gribin Ridge makes a superb descent route; the defined edge provides superb and exposed scrambling. The major difficulty is quickly reached in descent and involves reversing the rock steps. This should not, however, pose a major problem as the holds are large and obvious.

After the steps comes a sharp crest and some slabs. Beyond these the going changes from scrambling to walking on a large flat plateau. Continue along the obvious path until this splits to descend into either Cwm Bochlwyd or Cwm Idwal. In bad visibility be careful not to overshoot this junction and stray on to the crags of the Gribin Facet. From either of the cwms follow the paths to Ogwen Cottage and the road.

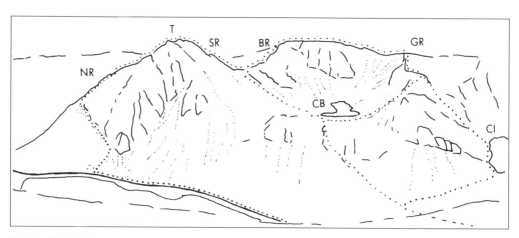

Tryfa –Glyder Traverse. NR – North Ridge; T – Tryfan (summit); SR – South Ridge; BR – Bristly Ridge; GR – Gribin Ridge; CB – Cwm Bochlwyd; CI – Cwm Idwal

Route 13

EAST GULLY ARÊTE

Mountain: Glyder Fach (994m)
Category: Scrambling and winter route
Grades: Scrambling – 3; climbing – Moderate; winter – II
Time: 4–5hrs
Distance: 5km
Height: 150m
Approach: GR 650 603; Ogwen Cottage
Route: GR 656 586
Maps: OS 1:25,000 Outdoor Leisure sheet 17; OS 1:50,000 Landranger sheet 115

Introduction: East Gully Arête provides a satisfyingly direct and central route up the impressive looking headwall that forms the north-west face of Glyder Fach. It connects a series of bold ribs and is often exposed, but it has lots of sound holds and marvellously rough rock that provides plenty of grip. Some of the moves, however, are quite exposed and would be difficult when wet.

Situation: The north-west face of Glyder Fach rises abruptly above Llyn Bochlwyd; it is bounded in the east by Bristly Ridge and in the west by Gribin Ridge. The centre of the face is dominated by Alphabet Slabs and the adjacent East Gully, which rises to the right of and then directly above the slabs. East Gully Arête follows a traverse above the slabs to gain the left-hand edge of the gully that it then follows directly to the summit slopes of Glyder Fach.

Approach: Leave the car park at Ogwen Cottage and follow the well-marked Cwm Idwal path. After 250m strike off south east along the indeterminate trail that leads to Cwm Bochlwyd. A more obvious path soon emerges as the peat bog is crossed and becomes well-defined as you start to climb the rock band that bars the entrance to Cwm Bochlwyd.

The path follows the course of Llyn Bochlwyd's outflow and soon steepens, eventually disappearing amongst the boulder field that blocks the entrance to the cwm. Once into the cwm the north-west face of Glyder Fach is obvious. Follow the eastern shore of the lake to the back of the cwm and to the east of the base of Alphabet Slabs, which rises above some considerable scree slopes.

Ascent: The route starts at the extreme left-hand edge of the base of Alphabet Slabs. Hereabouts is also the base of Main Gully which bounds the slabs on the left. Ascend Main Gully for about 25m until a quartz-pocked gangway is gained, then traverse right and above Alphabet Slabs to gain a sloping platform at the base of the ridge.

At the base of the ridge is a bulge that is awkward to negotiate. This move overlooks East Gully and is both exposed and intimidating. Take confidence from the knowledge that the holds are good, the rock sound and the friction superb. Nevertheless this is a move that should be fully protected with a belay.

Beyond the bulge is an obvious notch, with two ribs rising above – ascend the left-hand one. Above are a series of steep blocks that can be ascended on good holds. The sense of exposure is emphasized by the depth of East Gully and the ground remains steep.

The crux is soon reached: this is a steep wall split by a crack suitably sized for hand jamming. The ascent of the crack is far from straightforward and is not the end of the 'fun', for the wall is

53

East Gully Arête

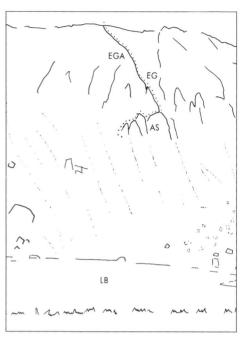

EGA – East Gully Arête; EG – East Gully;
AS – Alphabet Slabs;LB – Llyn Bochlwyd

topped by a mantleshelf. If this proves too much then it can be avoided by traversing to the right into the gully and then bypassing the crux to rejoin the route further up.

The going now eases and what difficulties there are can either be taken on directly or negotiated to one side or the other. As it ascends, the ridge trends to the left and overlooks Chasm Face and Main Gully. All too soon the crest merges with the main mountain and you come to the summit plateau and Glyder Fach.

Descent: From Glyder Fach the paths across the plateau provide several options for descent. The most direct is to descend via Gribin Ridge. The top of the ridge is 500m due west of the summit and is reached by following the path that skirts the top of the crags of the Cwm Bochlwyd headwall. Care should be taken in bad visibility and it should be noted that the path curves to the south before regaining its western heading.

You will have a choice of paths on Gribin Ridge and can either follow the walkers' path on the western flank or scramble along the crest. Both lead to a flat plateau and the well-trodden paths that return to Ogwen Cottage either via Cwm Idwal or Cwm Bochlwyd.

Route 14

DOLMEN RIDGE

Mountain: Glyder Fach (994m)
Category: Scrambling and winter route
Grades: Scrambling – 2/3; climbing – Easy; winter – II
Time: 5hrs
Distance: 6km
Height: 230m
Approach: GR 650 603; Ogwen Cottage
Route: GR 653 585
Maps: OS 1:25,000 Outdoor Leisure sheet 17; OS 1:50,000 Landranger sheet 115

Introduction: When seen from Cwm Bochlwyd the north-west face of Glyder Fach presents an impressive and intimidating prospect. The first impression is one of impregnability – nevertheless the lines of weakness are there even if they are not immediately apparent.

One of the more obvious features on the face is the Dolmen Buttress. Its right-hand edge provides a rising traverse that leads directly to the Glyder plateau just below the summit of Glyder Fach. The edge is known as Dolmen Ridge. For its grade it is not technically demanding, nevertheless it has a fine sense of atmosphere and a fair degree of exposure.

Situation: Glyder Fach's steep north-west face forms the headwall of Cwm Bochlwyd and rears over the resident Llyn. The face is contained on either flank by Bristly Ridge and Gribin Ridge. Dolmen Ridge is found well to the western side of the face and is defined by Central Gully (also known as Western Gully) and by Dolmen Buttress, whose upper right-hand edge forms the ridge.

Access to the base of the ridge is provided by Central Gully and this allows the steeper rocks of Dolmen Buttress to be bypassed. The lower reaches of the gully are, however, particularly unpleasant (unless they are snow filled) and the normal route avoids this by using a rising traverse on the other edge (right-hand side) of the gully.

Once on to the ridge the crest is narrow and quite exposed, particularly in its lower reaches. As you ascend, the angle eases and the crest becomes broken as the ridge joins the main mountain. There are, however, some interesting rock terraces which while optional do provide an athletic finale to the route; it terminates almost at the summit of Glyder Fach.

Approach: Leave the car park at Ogwen Cottage and follow the well-marked Idwal path. After 250m strike south along the indeterminate trail that leads to Cwm Bochlwyd; a more obvious path soon emerges as the peat bog is crossed and becomes well defined as you start to climb the rock band that bars the entrance to the Cwm.

This path soon steepens, eventually to disappear amongst the boulder field that fills the entrance to Cwm Bochlwyd; however, Llyn Bochlwyd soon emerges and, beyond, the north-west face of Glyder Fach.

Follow the shore of Llyn Bochlwyd round to the west and cross the major gully and boulder field that is formed by the junction of Gribin Ridge and Glyder Fach. A small pool at GR 653 586 (only marked on the OS 1:25,000 sheet) provides a useful reference point.

From the pool the triangular feature that is Dolmen Buttress is the main indicator for the start of the route. This lies west of centre on the face and well up the headwall above the scree slopes. The other indicator is Central Gully – this is an obvious gash on the face and

Dolmen Ridge

defines the western edge of Dolmen Buttress.

Ascent: Avoid going into the base of the gully, but seek out the slabs and terraces to the right of the gully. They are crossed by a series of quartz intrusions and should be obvious. Ascend first to the right and then gain a leftward traverse along the next slab.

Move left along the slab with an awkward move across a quartz vein and into a corner crack which can be ascended directly.

Entry to Central Gully is now possible where it narrows and on the opposite side is the start of Dolmen Ridge. Ascend the gully for a further 5m until the crest of the ridge can be gained via a steep slab over good holds.

Beyond the slab is a groove barred by a large boulder which can be overcome by airy climbing moves or resorting to

caving. Above, the crest of the ridge can now be followed with relative ease and the scrambling is fun rather than serious. The ridge proper comes to an end at a small col at the top of Western Gully, as the ridge merges with the main mountain.

Here there is a choice of routes: some easy and some which are much more challenging, involving athletic moves up a fine detached slab and pronounced cracks. Although the rock is a joy to move over, care should be taken as there are lots of loose boulders. Eventually you emerge on to the Glyder plateau with an easy walk to the summit of Glyder Fach.

Descent: From the summit of Glyder Fach the paths across the Glyder plateau provide several options for descent. The most direct is to descend via the Gribin Ridge. The top of the

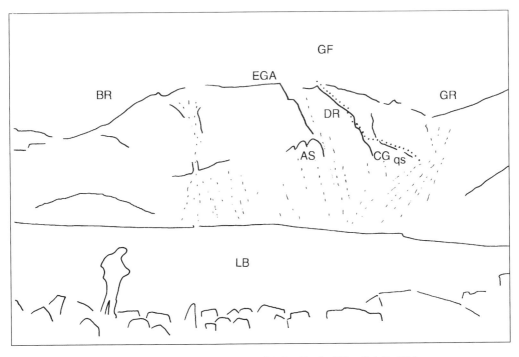

DR – Dolmen Ridge; CG – Central Gully; GF – Glyder Fach; BR – Bristly Ridge;
GR – Gribin Ridge; AS – Alphabet Slabs; LB – Llyn Bochlwyd; qs – quartz slabs

ridge is 500m due west of the summit and is reached by following the path that skirts the top of the crags of the Cwm Bochlwyd headwall. Care should be taken in bad visibility and it should be noted that the path curves to the south before resuming its westerly heading.

You will have a choice of paths on Gribin Ridge and can either follow the walkers' path on the western flank or scramble along the crest. Both lead to a flat plateau and the well-marked paths that return to Ogwen Cottage either via Cwm Idwal or Cwm Bochlwyd.

Route 15

CNEIFION ARÊTE

Mountains: Glyder Fach (994m) and Glyder Fawr (999m)
Category: Scrambling/rock climb and winter route
Grades: Scrambling – 3s; climbing – Moderate; winter – III
Time: 4–5hrs
Distance: 4km
Height: 140m
Approach: GR 650 603; Ogwen Cottage
Route: GR 648 588
Maps: OS 1:25,000 Outdoor Leisure sheet 17; OS 1:50,000 Landranger sheet 115

Introduction: The Climbers Club guide to Ogwen describes Cneifion Arête as 'a route reminiscent of the Alps' and grades it as a moderate rock climb. It is an exposed and razor-sharp arête that provides a bold and direct line; fortunately it also has lots of excellent holds, straightforward moves and sound belays if needed. Both the arête and the surroundings are impressive.

Situation: Cneifion Arête takes its name from Cwm Cneifion, a wild and remote hanging valley, high on the northern flank of the Glyders. It nestles between Gribin Ridge and Senior's Ridge and is invisible from the Ogwen Valley. Shown on the OS map with its English

Cneifion Arête

translation – 'Unnamed Cwm' – it is not the easiest place to reach as its entrance lies above the crags of the Sub-Cneifion Rib.

Cneifion Arête ascends directly from the floor of the cwm up the western flank of Gribin Ridge and emerges on a plateau just below where the rock crest of that ridge emerges. The arête appears as an obvious rock rib: to its right a pronounced gully, to the left a broken and open face. The start is easily identified by a large grass platform which lies atop some scree and directly below the first rock step of the arête.

Approach: From Ogwen Cottage car park take the Llyn Idwal path to the outflow. Pick up the path on the east side of the lake and follow this towards Idwal Slabs. Well before the slabs, ascend south east over the steep hillside towards the entrance of the cwm which is shown by a small waterfall (the flow is seasonal so do not rely on this feature in summer). A number of faint paths become apparent as you ascend, and if you trend to the south you can identify a break in the skyline formed by a gully. Scramble over well-worn rocks, up, into and out of this gully to gain the floor of Cwm Cneifion.

Ascent: Above the grass shelf you will

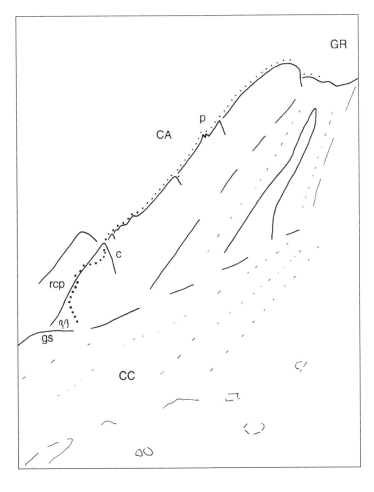

CA – Cneifion Arête;
CC – Cwm Cneifion;
GR – Gribin Ridge;
gs – grass shoulder;
rcp – rock climbing pitch;
c – chimney;
p – pinnacles

be able to see the first pitch which is the 'rock climb'. Although only graded Moderate it is about 30m in height and relatively steep with one slightly awkward move, so it would be worth belaying and fixing some protection.

Ascend the rock step on good holds, move left and then right to gain the base of a chimney. You can either climb the chimney directly or go up its more exposed left-hand edge. Once clear of the chimney the crest of the arête proper can be gained.

From here the going eases but it still remains very exposed, and depending on the party's experience, it probably will not be necessary to fully belay each section; however, this is an ideal place to employ the technique of moving together on a rope. There are plenty of good spikes for sling belays.

The next 15m follows the main crest on excellent holds and is then followed by a more broken section. After this the crest returns and some bold but easy moves can be enjoyed stepping across the tops of a series of spikes. This may not be a genuine crux, but it is a position to savour.

After the spikes, the crest starts to break up but the moves are still quite exposed. Some 120m above the top of the chimney the ground falls away and you emerge on to the open ground of Gribin Ridge.

Descent: The most direct route back to the road is to turn north and descend via the path along the lower section of Gribin Ridge before dropping down into either Cwm Idwal or Cwm Bochlwyd and then to the road. Care should be taken not to stray too far down Gribin Ridge and on to the crags of the Gribin Facet, but both paths are well worn.

The upper section of Gribin Ridge can be readily added to this route to extend the day (see Route 12: Gribin Ridge).

Route 16

EAST ARÊTE OF GLYDER FAWR

Mountain: Glyder Fawr (999m)
Category: Rock climb
Grades: Scrambling – N/A; climbing – Moderate; winter – N/A
Time: 6hrs
Distance: 6.5km
Height: 210m
Approach: GR 650 603; Ogwen Cottage
Route: GR 644 586
Maps: OS 1:25,000 Outdoor Leisure sheet 17; 1:50,000 Landranger sheet 115

Introduction: The massive headwall of Cwm Idwal is an impressive and complex feature. It is split into two distinct areas: the great sweep of Idwal Slabs and the remote looming rocks of the Upper Cliff of Glyder Fawr. The 'Slabs' are convenient and contain a number of classic lower-grade rock climbs. Consequently there is a vast amount of traffic; queuing is a fact of life for any one climbing here.

In contrast the Upper Cliffs are remote and involve a grinding approach but maintain a high mountain atmosphere. East Arête follows a straightforward but very enjoyable line to the Glyder Plateau up these fine cliffs and in a superb situation.

As a 'Moderate' it lies at the boundary between upper-grade scrambling and a mountaineering rock climb. *Do not, however, underestimate this route as a climb; in places the holds are often small, the climbing is quite delicate and often sustained. Furthermore, placing protection can be problematic.*

Situation: At the back of Cwm Idwal lies a vast area of rock divided into two distinct tiers. The cliffs are enclosed by Senior's Ridge in the east and the Devil's Kitchen in the west. The rock is distinctly aligned and produces a series of layered slabs, of which Idwal Slabs are the best example. This alignment is repeated on the Upper Cliffs.

East Arête follows the edge of one of these layers. To the left the rock drops away steeply to East Gully and an area of rock known as the Grey Group. To the right is the open slab of East Buttress. The first part of the arête consists of a rock step, while above ascends a quite broad but pinnacled crest.

Approach: The walk in falls into two distinct halves: a pleasant stroll into Cwm Idwal and a grinding toil up the scree below the cliffs. Leave Ogwen Cottage and follow the well-trodden path into Cwm Idwal. Go round the eastern side of the lake and skirt below the Idwal Slabs and beyond them for 100m to gain the wide scree slope which is ascended directly to the base of the cliffs.

Ascent: East Arête is off to the left of Central Gully which is easily identified as it is the lowest point on the base of the crag. Turn left and follow the base of the slabs that form East Buttress until another major gully is gained. This is East Gully and forms the left-hand edge of the arête.

The first pitch is up a compact rock step. It starts off quite steeply but can be avoided by traversing in from the left. If the direct approach is taken be prepared for some delicate, exposed and sustained moves. Either way gain a series of narrow quartz-pocked ledges. If the step is taken directly it should be pitched and fully belayed – smaller nuts and chockstones are useful.

The arête proper now rises above with a series of pinnacles emerging as

East Arête of Glyder Fawr East

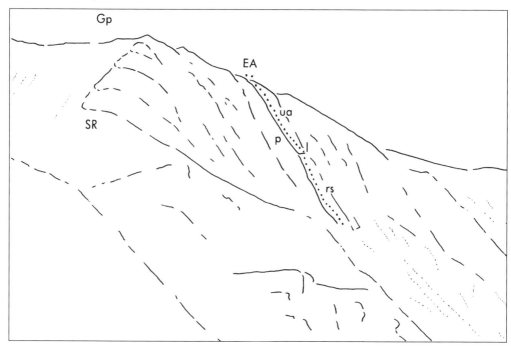

EA – East Arête; Gp – Glyder plateau; SR – Senior's Ridge; rs – rock step; l – ledges;
p – pinnacles; ua – upper arête

you ascend. Stick to the left at first but the arête soon becomes sufficiently straightforward to allow a choice of routes. Although the going now becomes easier, remain roped until you arrive on the Glyder plateau. Glyder Fawr lies some 300m to the south.

Descent: There are several routes off the Glyder plateau including the Devil's Kitchen path. The most convenient and interesting, however, is to descend via the Gribin Ridge. The top of this lies some 900m almost due east and is reached by skirting round the top of Cwm Cneifion. In descent there are two options: the first is to stick closely to the crest which is quite sporting; the second is to drop down to the west and use the walkers' path.

Eventually the ridge broadens and it is simply a matter of following the path until it splits at the top of the Bochlwyd Buttress. The choice is now to descend to either Cwm Idwal which is steeper but more direct or into Cwm Bochlwyd which is longer but easier on the knees. Both lead back to Ogwen Cottage by well-established paths.

Route 17

CENTRAL ARÊTE OF GLYDER FAWR

Mountain: Glyder Fawr (999m)
Category: Rock climb
Grades: Scrambling – N/A; climbing – Difficult; winter – N/A
Time: 6hrs
Distance: 6.5km
Height: 190m
Approach: GR 650 603; Ogwen Cottage
Route: GR 643 585
Maps: OS 1:25,000 Outdoor Leisure sheet 17; 1:50,000 Landranger sheet 115

Introduction: As with East Arête, Central Arête follows a straightforward and very enjoyable line to the Glyder plateau up these fine cliffs. *This time, however, the route is more technical and should be regarded as a full-blown mountaineering rock climb. Consequently, it is essential that each pitch is fully belayed and protected.*

Situation: At the back of Cwm Idwal lies a vast area of rock divided into two distinct tiers. The cliffs are enclosed by Senior's Ridge in the east and the Devil's Kitchen in the west. The rock is distinctly aligned and produces a series of layered slabs, of which Idwal Slabs are the best example. This alignment is repeated on the Upper Cliffs.

Central Arête follows the edge of one of these layers, the upper section forming a well-defined and toothed ridge. To the left the rock drops away steeply to open slabs. To the right is more broken ground consisting of narrow slabs and a series of gullies. The first section consists of a series of slabs that require

Central Arête of Glyder Fawr

delicate technique. They provide access to the arête proper, which consists of a well-defined crest and a series of exposed pinnacles.

Approach: As for Route 16.

Ascent: Seek out Central Gully, which lies adjacent to and on the right of the great sweep of slabs that form Eastern Buttress. To the right of Central Gully lies a second, narrower slab. To the right and above this lies a defined crest – this is Central Arête.

Start beneath and just to the right of the buttress, next to the narrow slab. Ascend a series of slabs for 45m to a grass ledge. The crux comes next, so belay here. Above can be seen an arête – move around to the right and climb a

slab on small holds. Technique and delicate movement are the key here. Although the holds appear minute they never give out and after 30m lead to a groove, which provides a welcome belay.

The going now eases and the crest of the arête can be reached. Ascend this using the left-hand side of the feature. After 17m, it is easier to move to the crest of the arête and this is ascended via a series of gendarmes and pinnacles for the remaining 100m. The situation is now straightforward, but it is exposed so the rope must still be used. The route leads directly to broken ground below the Glyder plateau.

Descent: As for Route 16

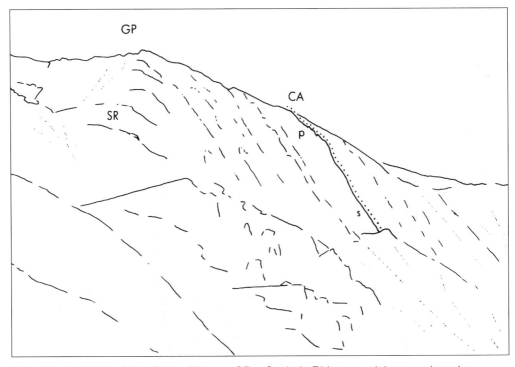

CA – Central Arête; GP – Glyder Plateau; SR – Senior's Ridge; s – slabs; p – pinnacles

Route 18

THE TRAVERSE OF Y GARN

Mountain: Y Garn (947m)
Category: Scrambling and winter route
Grades:
1) East-North-East Ridge: Scrambling –
2/3; climbing – Easy; winter – II
2) North-East Ridge: Scrambling – 1;
climbing – N/A; winter – I

Time: 5hrs
Distance: 5km
Height: 400m
Approach: GR 650 603; Ogwen Cottage
Route: GR 641 597
Maps: OS 1:25,000 Outdoor Leisure
sheet 17; OS 1:50,000 Landranger sheet
115

Introduction: Y Garn dominates the
skyline above Ogwen Cottage and there
is no mistaking its 'armchair'-like

Traverse of Y Garn

appearance. The two ridges that form the arms of the aforementioned 'chair' both provide good scrambling – albeit of varying grades. In the upper grades, the East-North-East Ridge provides a challenging and quite technical ascent, and while the north-east ridge probably wouldn't warrant attention in itself, it does provide an airy descent that makes for a fine expedition. When combined, these two ridges provide a superb traverse of one of Ogwen Valley's most striking peaks.

Situation: Y Garn lies to the south west of Ogwen Cottage at the southern end of the western wall of Nant Francon; its 'armchair' outline is defined by the high and remote hanging valley of Cwm Clyd and its two eastern ridges. The East-North-East Ridge, which is the most southerly of the two, is formed by Cwm Clyd to the north and the immense buttress of Castell y Geifr and

YG – Y Garn;
ENE – East-North-East Ridge;
NE – North-East Ridge

Cwm Idwal to the south. The North-East Ridge is flanked by Cwm Cywion to the north and Cwm Clyd to the south. Llyn Clyd and a smaller unnamed lake nestle within the 'chair'.

Approach: From Ogwen Cottage follow the track to the outflow of Llyn Idwal. Cross the stepping stones to the north and western shore and follow the path to the footbridge which crosses the stream that flows from Cwm Clyd, then cross this and gain the southern bank. Although it is not obvious and there is no path you are now below the base of the East North Ridge.

Ascent: Pick your own path across the initially level ground and head towards the rising ground and broken crags which should then be ascended. By trending left you will be able to make progress and, as you climb, the ridge will become more defined and a faint path can be discerned.

An obvious triangular-shaped rockface soon becomes apparent, but this should not be taken directly, for by passing it on the left you will be able to gain a gully that provides access to the top of the buttress. Nevertheless the going is exposed with more than its fair share of loose rock; do not hesitate to use a rope.

The top of the buttress is connected by a well-defined, slabbed and quite exposed ridge. Both flanks tumble steeply away to their respective cwms and there are two 4m steps to be negotiated. The sharp crest is terminated by a steep wall, with a mass of boulders at its base, which bars further movement along the main crest.

A route can be discerned traversing off to the left below the steep rocks and above Cwm Idwal. Foliow this until you reach a gully that provides about 30m of quite steep scrambling to regain the main crest. The going now eases for a while.

After a level traverse along the crest with only a small step to negotiate, another wall of vertically striated rock rears up. Trend right to reach some large blocks – the moves are relatively easy on good holds, but the exposure is considerable and all in all the situation is quite exciting. Eventually the ground falls away and all that is left is to clear some large boulders before gaining the grassy main summit ridge and summit of Y Garn after 500m.

Descent: After the rugged and exhilarating scrambling of the East-North-East Ridge, the North-East Ridge presents a slightly easier prospect. Nevertheless, it should be treated with respect for it is a narrow and exposed arête.

From the summit of Y Garn head north for 300m and then turn north east to descend directly down the narrow crest of the ridge, which although exposed has no major obstacles to overcome. The initial steep section of the ridge levels slightly after 75m, until a subsidiary top is reached from where a steep and winding path can be followed to regain the outflow at Llyn Idwal and the main track back to Ogwen Cottage.

Route 19

NEEDLE'S EYE ARÊTE

Mountain: Foel Goch (831m)
Category: Scrambling and winter route
Grades: Scrambling – 2/3; climbing – N/A; winter – III
Time: 5hrs
Distance: 7.5km
Height: 150m
Approach: GR 641 611 – cattle grid; alternative GR 650 603 – Ogwen Cottage
Route: GR 635 610
Maps: OS 1:25,000 Outdoor Leisure sheet 17; OS 1:50,000 Landranger sheet 115

Introduction: Such is the quality of so many of the routes around Ogwen Cottage that seclusion is a seldom realized aspect of mountaineering in the Glyders. Foel Goch benefits greatly from being just outside the main orbit of the Ogwen Valley and it enjoys a real sense of isolation. This is not all this route has to offer, however, for it is a challenging and attractive scramble that is also quite serious in places. It has great potential as a winter route.

Situation: The northern wing of the Glyders forms the western wall of Nant Francon. High up on this wall is the summit of Foel Goch and the hanging valley of Cwm-coch. Needle's Eye Arête is to be found on the left-hand side of Creigiau Gleision, the crag which forms the northern flank of the mountain's southern ridge.

The arête consists of a series of jagged pinnacles that rise above the northern wall of the prominent Eastern Gully. It is this gully which provides both access to the route and indicates the start when viewed from the cwm; for the arête – so obvious from Ogwen – merges with the confusion of rock that is Creigiau Gleision when seen from directly below.

Approach: Leave the minor road, which branches off from the A5 at Ogwen Cottage and passes directly in front of the youth hostel, at the cattle grid through the farm gate on the west side. On the hillside above can be seen two water courses (marked on the map as streams, but both dry up quickly); follow the right-hand bank of the north one into Cwm-coch. At the 500m contour the ground levels as the upper cwm is reached – turn south and traverse by a path across the base of the Creigiau Gleision.

It is easier to identify Needle's Eye Arête by picking out the gully. This is found at the eastern (left-hand) edge of the crag and is marked by an obvious erosion scar where the path breaks the skyline. Below the path a complex of dry stone walls and sheep folds can be seen. Just in from this you should be able to pick up a large gully, known as Eastern Gully. The arête is the rib which bounds it on the right.

Ascent: The arête is gained by ascending the gully for about 10m until your way is blocked by a mossy rock step. Turn this to the right on grassy ledges and then move back left to the top of it. The arête can now be seen off to the right as a series of ascending and jagged pinnacles.

The next section is awkward rather than difficult. Move right for 9m to gain the base of the tower, easily identified by a small 'window' formed by two large rocks that jam a smaller one. The next sequence is quite tricky and involves a delicate traverse under the overhanging bulge at the base of the tower. The handholds are mostly firm but the footholds are decidedly dubious – good enough

Needle's Eye Arête

reason for using a rope! Once around this corner, a small heather-filled gully now provides access to a notch just below the arête proper.

The route now takes on a glorious alpine feel and ascends an airy slab to a short but very sharp knife-edge. This can be negotiated by balance or by sitting astride it 'a cheval'. Above the edge you will be able to identify an obvious hole through the crest of the ridge. This is the 'Needle's Eye', which not only gives the arête its name but – if you have sufficient slings – also provides a sound belay to bring your partner up on!

Atop the Needle's Eye lies a series of dubiously balanced blocks – these could be taken direct but the moves are particularly intimidating. A more feasible alternative is to traverse to the left along a heather gangway and then ascend a short wall to regain the main crest.

The going now starts to ease and you can look forward to some straightfor-

ward but airy scrambling along an exposed ridge. Next come two pinnacles which are best if taken direct and they are then followed by a noticeably larger pinnacle. The key to this feature is to ascend the groove which cuts the face in two.

All that is left after the last pinnacle is a short section of grassy arête complete with a few rock spikes and then a rock step split into two levels. The lower tier is slightly overhanging, but luckily this is blessed with good positive holds and a bit of determination will soon overcome it. Above this, the ground falls away and Needle's Eye Arête and Eastern Gully merge as the eastern ridge of Foel Goch is gained.

Descent: The summit lies some 600m to the north west and is easily gained via the col at Bwlch y Cywion. From the top of Foel Goch your onward route is somewhat limited. The ridge that

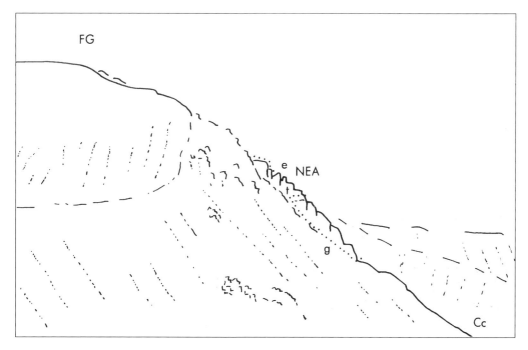

NEA – Needle's Eye Arête; FG – Foel Goch; Cc – Cwm-coch;
g – gully; t – terrace; e – eye (of the needle)

descends north eastward directly from the summit – marked on the map as Yr Esgair – is definitely not a safe option for descent.

The most direct option is to return to the col at Bwlch y Cywion, descend via the scree run to Cwm-coch and then pick up your outward route. A more ele-gant option – which would make Ogwen Cottage the best start point with a walk to the cattle grid – is to follow the ridge round to 300m short of the sum-mit of Y Garn (947m) and descend down the North-East Ridge (see Route 18: The Traverse of Y Garn).

Route 20

YR ESGAIR

Mountain: Foel Goch (831m)
Category: Winter route
Grades: Scrambling – N/A; climbing –
N/A; winter – II/III
Time: 4–5hrs
Distance: 3km
Height: 331m
Approach: GR 641 611 – cattle grid;
alternative GR 650 603 – Ogwen Cottage
Route: GR 632 613
Maps: OS 1:25,000 Outdoor Leisure
sheet 17; OS 1:50,000 Landranger sheet
115

Introduction: Yr Esgair is usually given
a wide berth by most sensible parties. It
has a bad reputation because of a 15m
band of appallingly loose rock that separates the lower ridge – which is a
superb knife-edge – from the upper
arête. This barrier is exposed, steep,
consists of loose rock and lacks any
form of sound belays or reasonable protection – horrendous.

In normal conditions, the options on
either side of the arête are hardly more
appealing. To the left, a series of steep,
loose and exposed slabs; to the right, a
descent into a gully provides access to a
more viable but often unpleasantly wet
corner and a friable, turf-riven wall.
Above, the upper arête is relatively
straightforward, but is also made up of a
mixture of unreliable rock and heather.

Nevertheless, the Yr Esgair has much
to commend it for it is a fine, direct line
that breaches an impressive headwall
and leads directly to a summit. The surroundings are magnificent, the setting
remote and unfrequented.

The key to a successful and relatively
safe ascent is in waiting for full winter
conditions with consolidated snow, and

then going for an early start. Then, the
right-hand approach – with the gully
and corner banked with snow and the
wall sufficiently frozen to provide a
semblance of solidity – becomes an
enjoyable challenge rather than a desperate epic.

The upper ridge also benefits from a
good covering of snow, as the broken
ground is bonded and covered. All
in all, winter conditions transform the
Yr Esgair into a classic route. Unfortunately, sustained winter conditions
are rare in Snowdonia.

Situation: Yr Esgair is the north-east
ridge of Foel Goch and overlooks the
south side of Nant Ffrancon to the north
of Ogwen Cottage. The south flank is
formed by Cwm-coch, to the north
Cwm Perfedd; the headwalls of both
these cirques are unremitting, steep and
often hold loose rock.

From a flank, the upper and lower
sections of the ridge are apparent. The
lower is shaped like a whaleback and is
knife-edged. The lower section is separated from the rest of the ridge and the
mountain itself by a deep gap – the top
of Esgair Gully. The problem arête is
above this break in the skyline. This is
steep, narrow and very loose. Above the
arête is a pronounced shoulder, with the
remainder of the ridge ascending above
at a steady 45 degrees that leads directly to the summit of Foel Goch.

Approach: Leave the minor road, which
branches off the A5 at Ogwen Cottage
and goes directly in front of the Youth
Hostel, at the cattle grid. Go through the
gate on the western side of the road and
ascend the water course into Cwm-coch.
Yr Esgair forms the north wall of the
cwm. From here, the approach to the
start of the ridge is apparent and
straightforward.

Yr Esgair

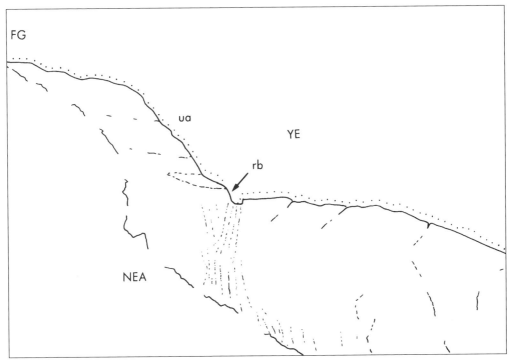

YE – Yr Esgair; FG Foel Goch; NEA – Needle's Eye Arête; ke – knife-edge;
rb – rock band; ua – upper arête

Traverse/ascent: Gain the broad eastern end of the ridge and follow the crest, which soon narrows to a knife-edge. This presents no major difficulties; it is simply a matter of enjoying the experience. This comes to an end at the notch.

Descend into the notch. The arête rears sickeningly above – do not be fooled into attempting it; the difficulties get worse as you ascend. There is no protection nor belay points on the arête, so a rope is of very little use. The consequences of a fall would be serious.

Look to the right and descend into the gully for 8m, where you will be able to gain a corner. If, as is advised, you are following the route when it is covered in snow, this will be a delicate exercise on crampons. If not, then it can be an unpleasant thrutch. Likewise, frozen turf and the ice-bound rock above provide a degree of security which is normally lacking. Ascend the corner, and then the wall, to gain a ledge trending to the right, and then move back towards the main crest to arrive at an obvious

shoulder on the main ridge. The worst is now behind.

The ridge can now be ascended directly and it is simply a matter of sticking to the crest. Care should be taken as the exposure is considerable and there is the continuing problem of loose rock, turf and little in the way of protection. Again the route is transformed with a covering of well-packed snow. The upper ridge ends at the summit.

Descent: From the summit of Foel Goch you have access to the long ridge that forms the west wall of Nant Ffrancon. All routes north require a long and circuitous descent. The most direct descent is via Easy Gully, located 250m to the south east of the summit. This steep but manageable scree chute requires care. It will quickly return you to Cwm-coch and then the outward path. A more elegant alternative is to follow the main ridge south for 1.75km and descend via the North-East Ridge of Y Garn

The Carneddau

Route 21 – Horned Ridge
Route 22 – The Llech Ddu
Spur

Approaches: A5 to Betws-y-Coed, Ogwen Cottage and Bethesda. Rail and bus link to Conway, Bangor and Betws-y-Coed. Bus link from Betws-y-Coed to Bethesda, but this is limited outside the summer.

Accommodation: Camping – Established sites in the Ogwen Valley; youth hostels – Idwal Cottage (at Ogwen Cottage) and Capel Curig; B&B and hotels – Capel Curig and Bethesda.

Tourist Information: 01690 710665.

Route 21

HORNED RIDGE

Mountain: Pen Yr Ole Wen (978m)

Category: Scrambling and winter route
Grades: Scrambling – 2; climbing – N/A; winter – II
Time: 5hrs
Distance: 6km
Height: 380m
Approach: GR 650 603; Ogwen Cottage
Route: GR 648 609
Maps: OS 1:25,000 Outdoor Leisure sheet 17; OS 1:50,000 Landranger sheet 115

Introduction: The Horned Ridge of Pen Yr Ole Wen has probably attracted more people to scrambling than any other route in this book. A photograph of a section of this ridge, complete with a spectacularly poised climber, adorned the front of Steve Ashton's *'Scrambles in Snowdonia'*, the guidebook that generated so much interest in scrambling fifteen years ago.

Regrettably, and although the route does contain some very spectacular sections, it does not quite live up to the promise of that photograph. The main drawback is that the series of ribs and pinnacles which make up the line of the ridge are both broken and discontinuous. Most notably the line of the ridge disappears at mid-height and involves a tedious ascent over scree and heather. Nevertheless, the quality of those sections that stand proud from the main face do justify its inclusion.

Situation: Pen Yr Ole Wen rears above Ogwen Cottage, presenting a uniformly steep and intimidating prospect. The ascent by its South Ridge must be one of the most tedious grinds in Britain's mountains. The Braich Ty Du Face lies to the west of the ridge and is made up of a series of rock ribs and vegetated gullies. A band of scree runs at mid-height across the face.

The Horned Ridge lies just to the west of the South Ridge, starting from just above the road, apart from the mid-height band of scree and heather, and leads up to the summit area. In its most spectacular sections, it consists of a narrow crest of spikes and small pinnacles complete with lots of exposure.

Approach: Leave Ogwen Cottage and follow the A5 over the bridge that crosses the Afon Ogwen at the outflow from Llyn Ogwen. Follow the right-hand side of the road until the Alfred Embleton stile is reached.

Cross the stile and ascend the South Ridge path until a series of zig-zags is reached. Traverse to the left below the first buttress and then across a gully to gain an obvious and well-defined rock ridge. This is the start of Horned Ridge.

Ascent: Go into the gully to the right of the ridge and scramble to a stone wall; 10m above the wall is a grass rake which provides access to the crest of the ridge. Once on the crest the way is barred by a rock step 3m in height, so go to the right and ascend on good holds to a ledge.

Above lies a superb pinnacled ridge in classic saw-toothed configuration. Traverse this at will, but most problems arise on the right flank overlooking the gully. Far too soon superb scrambling gives way to a grassy col and the band of heather and scree that crosses the face.

To see the next section of the route, look up and left beyond the band to a series of curving ribs. Approach them initially via a gully and then by a series of low outcrops to avoid the worst of the scree.

Gain the first rib and ascend to the crest; after a few metres the route gets serious and sanctuary must be sought in the gully to the left. Cross this and gain a second rib. Ascend a vegetated groove to gain the crest proper after 24m.

Stick to the crest as far as possible, though detours will need to be sought to avoid holdless rock. The knife-edge remains well defined but route finding can be complex when the holds run out. Eventually the ridge loses its definition and merges with the main mountain as the summit plateau is reached. Continue along the South Ridge path to the top of Pen Yr Ole Wen.

Descent: Unless forced to do so by worsening weather or fading light, avoid the descent by the South Ridge at all costs. Although it is straightforward, it is unpleasant and will exact a cost in wear and tear of knees and ankles. Better to descend via the East Ridge to the far end of Llyn Ogwen or opt for the delights of a walk into the Carneddau. A fine, though quite lengthy, option takes in Carnedd Dafydd, Carnedd Llewelyn, Pen Yr Helgi Du, returning to the Ogwen Valley via the Y Braich to Helyg and the road.

Horned Ridge

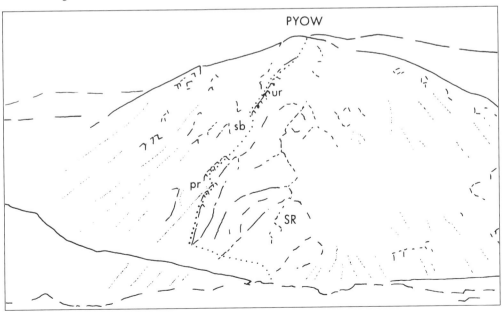

PYOW – Pen Yr Ole Wen; SR – South Ridge; pr – pinnacled ridge;
sb – scree band; ur – upper ribs

Route 22

THE LLECH DDU SPUR

Mountain: Carnedd Dafydd (1,044m)
Category: Scrambling and winter route
Grades: Scrambling – 1; climbing – N/A; winter – I
Time: 5–6hrs
Distance: 7.7km
Height: 200m
Approach: GR 638 659 – entrance to waterworks
Route: GR 664 637
Maps: OS 1:25,000 Outdoor Leisure sheet 17; OS 1:50,000 Landranger sheet 115

Introduction: The Carneddau is the largest mountain group in Wales. From their boundaries they often give an immediate impression of massive rounded bulk, rather than the complex landscape of cwm and ridge that is typical of much of Snowdonia. Yet these mountains should not be underestimated nor dismissed lightly; for in their heart lie some grand cirques and very impressive rock scenery.

In many respects the terrain is similar to the Cairngorms – a rolling plateau dissected by large glacial valleys and flanked by towering cliffs. As with the Cairngorms the weather can also be harsh and there is little shelter from the wind as it blasts over the exposed tops.

Tucked away in the western quadrant of the range lies a fine ridge – the Llech Ddu Spur. Although technically straightforward, its stature is greatly enhanced by the grandeur and feeling of isolation of Cwm Glas Llafar and the towering cliffs of Ysgolion Duon – one of the most atmospheric crags in Snowdonia.

Situation: Upper Cwm Llafar is split in two by the triangular-shaped crag of Llech Ddu (considered second only to Clogwyn D'ur Arddu for serious rock climbing in Snowdonia), which terminates the Llech Ddu Spur. To the east lies Cwmglas Mawr with its massive headwall of Ysgolion Duon and to the west the complex Cwmglas Bach.

The spur rises above Llech Ddu's northerly face and then ascends at a steady 45 degrees directly to the summit dome of Carnedd Dafydd. Although much of the route's quality is imparted by its magnificent situation, it is nevertheless both narrow and quite exposed in parts, if a little too grassy.

Approach: The walk -in starts at the end of the minor road that heads through Gwernydd to the south east of Bethesda by the entrance to the waterworks (care and consideration should be taken over parking). Cross the Afon Llafar and then go south and then south east around the perimeter fence of the waterworks (there is no right of way through the grounds).

At the south corner, a path that leads through some ruined buildings can be seen – follow this until you start picking up footpath markers; these lead to the path that follows the river into Cwm Llfar. After about 2.5km, the easily recognized triangle of Lech Ddu appears. Make for the obvious large boulders (built up with stone walls into a sheep fold, or, if you are desperate, a bivi) in the scree at the bottom of the crag.

Ascent: A faint path trends west through the scree – follow this between the right (western) edge of the crag and the obvious waterfall to gain access to the western flank of the spur. Make sure you are clear of the steep ground of the main face and sides of the face. Then ascend the easy grassy terraces of the

Llech Ddu Spur

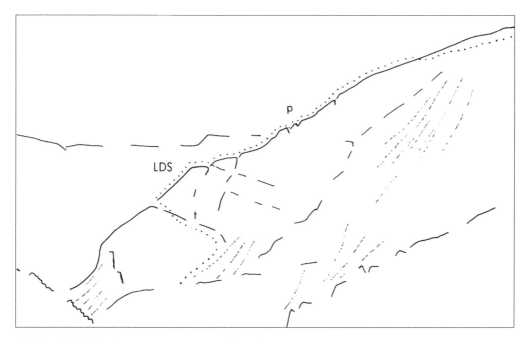

LDS – Llech Ddu Spur; t – terrace; p – pinnacles

flank until the main crest is gained.

Initially the spur is broad but it soon narrows and, although the rock is not continuous, the crest is barred by a series of smaller and two larger pinnacles. These are best taken directly, the largest having a sloping slab to descend on on its far side. This too is best taken directly although it will be intimidating if wet or iced up.

After the larger pinnacles, the spur abuts the main ridge and a large buttress appears; this can be tackled head on but there is an easier traverse off to the left. Both lead to the main ridge of Carnedd Dafydd, whose summit lies 200m to the south west.

Descent: Having gained the main ridge/plateau of the northern Carneddau, a number of long ridge walks are possible and an ascent/traverse of Carnedd Llwelyn (1,062m) and Yr Elen (962m) will provide good views of the Llech Ddu Spur and a good way to return to the start. The most direct route, however, is to descend via Carnedd Dafydd's north-west ridge and pick up the outward path.

The Lake District

The Lake District is England's major upland region and the only one that can be regarded as mountainous. The district holds all of England's four 3,000ft summits and the landscape bears the indelible mark of the action of ice. Long since vanished glaciers scoured out the deep valleys and the action of frost-thaw shattering created the deep corries – often known locally as coves – and the associated ridges, a few of which still maintain an alpine-like sharpness.

The Lake District's enormous influence on mountaineering and rock climbing bears no relationship to its modest altitude and size. Indeed it can be argued that the sport of rock climbing – as distinct from mountaineering – first saw the light of day with the ascent of Nape's Needle on Great Gable.

The Lakeland mountains also generated their own particular pursuit, that of fell walking. Named for the rounded terrain that typifies many of the district's mountains, known locally as fells, it involves long walks atop wide grassy ridges with little recourse to moving over rock. By tradition, it is the most gentle of mountain activities.

As a result, the gulf between walking on, and climbing up, mountains is more pronounced here than it is in Snowdonia and the Scottish Highlands, where nearly all summits require some movement over steep or exposed rock to gain a peak. This, unfortunately, had led to a perception that the Lake District has less to offer the mountaineer.

To dismiss the district on this basis is a major mistake. The three well-known edges – Striding, Swirrall and Sharp – provide a good introduction to mountaineering. There is, however, much more to do apart from these classics, and a wide range of routes provides a broad spectrum of challenge. Undoubtedly, in the Lakes a modicum of rock climbing skill will open up a much greater list of potential routes.

As an added bonus, the Lake District tends to hold snow cover longer than Snowdonia. As a result, in a typical winter there is far greater potential for routes that require the full range of alpine mountaineering skills.

Situation: All of the routes listed in this section lie within the Lake District National Park. The mountains on which they are found are all dissected by a series of valleys often filled with large lakes (and for which the district is named and famed). The layout of these valleys can simply be described as like the spokes of a wheel radiating from a core located around Esk Hause and adjacent to the district's highest peak, Scafell Pike.

The mountain ranges or fells lie between these valleys and are often located using the points of a compass with an additional grouping in the centre. This is the method used in this book, and this section is split into the following groups: Southern Fells; Western Fells; Central Fells; Northern

Fells and Far Eastern Fells.

The four highest peaks are Scafell Pike (977m) and its neighbour Scafell (964m), both located in the Western Fells, Helvellyn (950m) in the Eastern Fells, and Skiddaw (931), in the Northern Fells. Other significant peaks which hold fine routes are Great Gable, the Langdale Pikes, Pillar and Blencathra.

The distribution of the routes often reflects the quality of the rock, the best tending to lie to the south and the west of the district. However, this trend is counterbalanced to a degree in the north and east, which tend to hold their snow cover longer, so maintaining more 'alpine-like' conditions for longer during a typical winter.

Approaches: Many of the fells lie within an easy drive of the M6 motorway, although it can take much longer to reach the Western Fells. The region is well served by good roads, although this network and the car parks are coming under quite heavy pressure, particularly in the summer. There is a rail link to Windermere and a bus network of varying degrees of coverage.

The main towns are Windermere, Ambleside, Keswick, Whitehaven, Kendal and Penrith. These tend to be remote from the higher fells, but accommodation – youth hostels, campsites, B&B and a good spread of pubs – are to be found in all the major valleys close to the mountains and make for good bases.

Far Eastern Fells

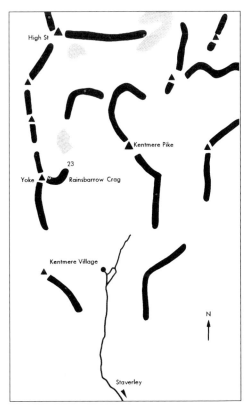

Route 23 – North-East Ridge of Rainsbarrow Crag

Approaches: A591 to Staveley. Rail and bus link to Kendal (Oxenholme) and Windermere. Kendal–Windermere bus, drop off at Staveley.

Accommodation: Camping – very limited camping on farm sites in Kentmere Valley (permission required) and rough camping on open fell; youth hostels – Kendal and Ambleside; B&B and hotels – Kendal, Kentmere, Staveley and Windermere.

Tourist information: 015394 32582.

Route 23

NORTH-EAST RIDGE OF RAINSBARROW CRAG

Mountain: Yoke (706m)
Category: Scrambling and winter route
Grades: Scrambling – 1; climbing – N/A: winter – I
Time: 4–5hrs
Distance: 8km
Height: 275m
Approach: GR 456 041; Kentmere Village
Route: GR 444 071
Maps: OS 1:25,000 Outdoor Leisure sheet 7; OS 1:50,000 Landranger sheet 90

Introduction: Harry Griffin is to Lake District mountaineering what Wainwright was to Lakeland fell walking. His regular articles in *The Guardian* and the *Lancashire Evening Post*, along with his many books, did much to define the pursuit we now call scrambling. This is one of his routes.

The Far Eastern Fells of Lakeland receive little coverage in scrambling guides and are regarded as having little potential by many people. This route does something to redress the balance. It is an excellent lower-grade scramble that climbs for almost 300m from just above the Kentmere Valley floor to the summit ridge of Yoke. The scrambling is very straightforward, but the upper ridge does narrow to a well-defined and exposed crest.

Situation: Lakeland's Far Eastern Fells stretch from the Kirkstone Pass road out

North-East Ridge of Rainsbarrow Crag

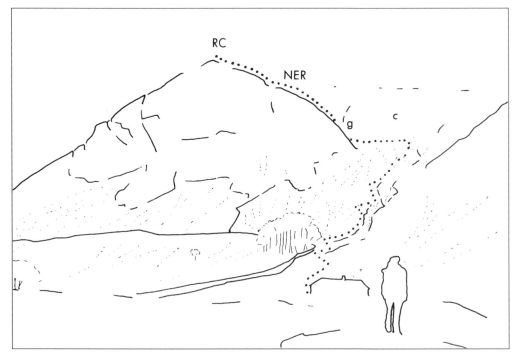

RC – Rainsbarrow Crag; NER – North-East Ridge; c – cove; g – gully

to the eastern border of the National Park. No road succeeds in actually crossing the high ground in between, so the footpaths are wild and remote. These mountains receive far fewer visitors than their western neighbours and retain a sense of isolation that has since disappeared in other parts of the district.

Yoke is found in the southern part of these fells overlooking the Kentmere Valley. Rainsbarrow Crag is a truncated spur that forms the eastern flank of the mountain and overlooks the upper valley. This ridge is found on the northern edge of the crag and is formed by Rainsbarrow Cove to the north west and the main face of the crag to the south.

The ridge rises from where the entrance to the cove meets the edge of the crag. The line of the route is obvious from below and the broader base soon gives way to an obvious crest. The rock is fairly continuous, if a little loose, and consists of a series of low towers. At the top of the ridge the edge gives way to a small plateau – complete with its own tarn – just below Yoke's summit.

Approach: From Kentmere Village follow the track, signposted for Hartrigg Farm, below Raven Crag and for 3km into the upper dale. Keep to the west of the River Kent and walk to the cluster of buildings marked on the map as Reservoir Cottages. Rainsbarrow Crag rises above the valley and will have been obvious for some time.

A stream issues from the cove above and descends between Rainsbarrow Crag and Steel Rig. Ascend alongside the stream to gain the entrance to the cove. Hereabouts look left and you will be able to see the ridge and identify the start of the crest.

Ascent: The lower reaches of the ridge consist of a steep and loose rock step which is best avoided. There are two alternatives. The easier is to ascend the hillside to the right of the rock and traverse in from above it. The second option, which is best left for good winter conditions when it is banked with snow, is to ascend a gully that cuts through the rock step.

Both lead to a shoulder on the ridge from where the crest can be followed. The going from here is very straightforward. In its early stages the ridge is quite broad and consists of a series of easily angled rock steps. These can be ascended or avoided pretty much at will. The rock is surprisingly good.

Eventually a much more defined crest emerges and there is little choice but to stick to it. The situation is also quite exposed with considerable drops on both flanks. Nevertheless the going remains straightforward and eventually the ridge leads to a small plateau, complete with tarn, just below the summit of Yoke, which lies 500m to the south west.

Descent: Yoke lies at the start of a well-known and lengthy fell walk – which in part follows the line of an old Roman road – called the Kentmere Round. Given sufficient time this can be followed and leads over Ill Bell (757m), High Street (828m), Mardale Ill Bell (750m) and Kentmere Pike (730m). This route can be shortened by dropping down to the valley from the summit of Nan Bield Pass.

The most direct return to the start point is to continue south over Yoke to Garburn Pass and then follow the pass via Crabtree Brow to Kentmere village.

Southern Fells

Route 24 – Steel Edge
Route 25 – Scafell Traverse

Approaches: A591 to Ambleside then A593 to Coniston, or A593 and Wrynose/Hardknott Pass to upper Eskdale. Regular bus link to Coniston from Kendal, Windermere and Ambleside. Rail link to Ravenglass from Lancaster and Carlisle. Daily service on the Ravenglass–Eskdale miniature railway (very limited in winter).

Accommodation: Camping – sites in and around Eskdale and Coniston; youth hostels – Eskdale, Coniston Coppermines and Holly How.

Tourist information: 01900 822634 and 015394 41533.

Route 24

STEEL EDGE

Mountain: Wetherlam (762m)
Category: Rough walking/scrambling and winter route
Grades: Scrambling – 1; climbing – N/A; winter – I
Time: 3–4hrs
Distance: 6km
Height: 250m
Approach: GR 307 009; National Trust car park
Route: GR 298 008
Maps: OS 1:25,000 Outdoor Leisure sheet 6; OS 1:50,000 Landranger sheet 90

Steel Edge

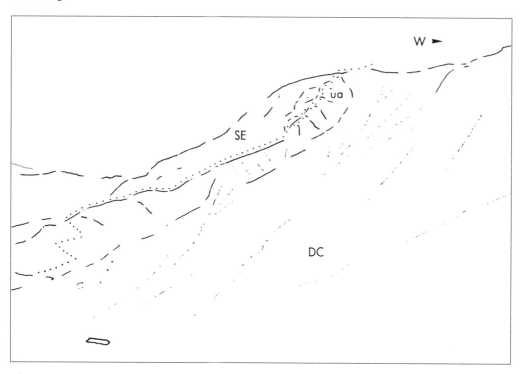

SE – Steel Edge; W – Wetherlam; DC – Dry Cove; ua – upper arête

Introduction: This route has little in the way of technical difficulties – in summer it is a very straightforward scramble, while under winter conditions it makes an ideal place for a first winter mountaineering route. In addition the approach is only a short walk, making it an ideal undertaking if time is limited. Nevertheless, both the route and the surroundings have a charm and grandeur that is typical of the Coniston Fells.

Situation: Wetherlam is the most easterly summit on the long ridge of the Coniston Fells. Like all of the other peaks in the range its flanks are deeply cut by deep cirques divided by rocky ridges. The hand of man is also apparent on this mountain, which has been subject to both quarrying and mining. Steel Edge is formed by Dry Cove to the north, and by the northern flanks of the Coniston valley to the south. The ridge is divided into three distinct sections: the lower portion is a broad but broken, rock ridge, the middle section narrows to a level ridge, and the upper section takes the form of a steepening arête. The rock can be loose, but there is insufficient exposure for this to become a serious problem.

Approach: From the car parks in Low Tilberthwaite, follow the signposted and prepared path along the southern side of Tilberthwaite Ghyll. This quickly leads to a plateau at the base of Steel Edge and the entrance to Dry Cove. Continue along the path to the entrance to Dry Cove.

Ascent: Steel Edge will have been apparent since the path cleared the upper reaches of Tilberthwaite Ghyll. Skirt round its base to gain the broad crest up its north-western flank. A series of paths winds amongst the small outcrops.

Once on the crest, it is simply a matter of following this upward. It quickly narrows to a well-defined edge. In summer this is covered in grass with an obvious path, so it presents no major challenge. In winter, however, it is a different matter and will require more care.

Eventually the level ridge steepens and gives way to the arête. The going becomes a little more demanding but is never too serious. A path does zig-zag between the outcrops and this can be followed at will. The arête emerges on to the south-eastern ridge of Wetherlam, which lies 900m to the north west and is gained via a broad but rocky ridge that skirts the top of Hen Crag.

Descent: From the top of Wetherlam a number of grand, wide-ranging fell walks can be followed. The main Coniston ridge lies off to the west and can be reached via Prison Band. The most direct route back to the road head is to descend north east from the summit via Wetherlam Edge to Birk Fell Hawse, before dropping down quickly to Dry Cove and the outward path. An alternative path exists on the northern rim of Tilberthwaite Ghyll and provides another perspective to this deep gorge.

Route 25

SCAFELL TRAVERSE

Cockly Pike Ridge and Mickledore/Broad Stand

Mountains: Ill Crag (935m), Scafell Pike (977m) and Scafell (964m)
Category: Primarily a scrambling (interspersed with extensive rough walking) and winter route
Grades: Scrambling – 1–3s; climbing – Difficult (short section only); winter – I
Time: 6–8+hrs
Distance: 17.5km
Height: 485m and 15m
Approach: GR 212 011; Lay-byes
Route: GR 229 070
Maps: OS 1:25,000 Outdoor Leisure sheets 4 and 6; 1:50,000 Landranger sheet 90 and 89

Introduction: The Scafell Range contains England's two highest peaks, Scafell Pike and Scafell; it also forms a massive and rugged ridge. Forming the core of the Cumbrian mountains, this massif, the neighbouring peaks and surrounding valleys do much to dispel the popularized image that the Lake District consists entirely of rolling fells and pleasant lake-filled dales. This is a remote and wild terrain that consists of fine mountains and isolated corries.

By linking together two ridges that are diverse in difficulty and character – Cockly Pike Ridge (grade 1) on Ill Crag and Mickledore/Broad Stand (grade 3s) on Scafell – along with some rugged high mountain walking, a fine traverse across England's highest peaks can be achieved. This route is adventurous, provides a genuine sense of wilderness and demands skill and commitment.

Situation: Cockley Pike Ridge provides

over 400m of pleasant but straightforward ascent. It rises from upper Eskdale above the wide-open tract of the Great Moss and forms the right-hand edge of the south-east face of Ill Crag. It breaks on to the top of Scafell Range just to the north east of Ill Crag which is a subsidiary summit below Scafell Pike.

Mickledore is the col between Scafell Pike and Scafell and appears to provide a direct route between the two summits. The top of the col forms a quite narrow crest – this, in itself, does not provide a major obstacle and is little more than a stroll, but it has a definite sting in the tail.

The ridge is blocked by a steep and exposed rock step where it abuts Scafell's rocky northern flank – this is the infamous Broad Stand. Its real danger lies not in its actual technical difficulty – the level is about Diff and does deserve respect – but in its apparent ease when seen from a distance.

This, along with it being the most obvious and direct route between the two summits, has tempted many parties to try it when they have neither the necessary skill or equipment. As a result many people have come to grief hereabouts. Nevertheless, for a reasonably skilled and properly equipped party it falls well short of being an insurmountable obstacle.

Approach: This route involves a long walk in, but it is through some of the Lake District's wildest and most spectacular scenery. Leave the Hardknott–Eskdale road at the bottom of the final steep section at the base of Hardknott Pass and pick up the signposted track that leads through the farm at Brotherikeld. Head north east following the eastern bank of the River Esk, crossing Lingcove Beck over the pack horse bridge.

Continue along the eastern bank of the River Esk above the fine gorge carved out by the river, and on to the Great Moss. Continue across this, then beyond Esk Buttress and Little Narrowcove. As you gain the upper reaches of Eskdale you will be able to identify the south-east face of Ill Crag and the ridge that forms the right-hand edge of the face. This is Cockly Pike Ridge.

Ascent/traverse: Beyond Little Narrowcove you should be able to identify a moraine ridge. Follow this across the boulder field to gain the ridge at the base of a knoll – Cockly Pike. Ascend this on the left and go on up a series of smaller pyramids until the summit of a promontory is gained.

The ridge is now barred by a rock barrier, so go past this to the left via a grass terrace and then ascend some quite steep rocks. After this is a depression and a mass of large boulders. Keep to the left and cross a scree chute and a grass terrace to gain an obvious rock rib. A slab trends to the right – ascend this and then head right to regain the rib.

Above, the chaos of boulder and scree continues but firm going can be found along a series of ribs. Continue atop these for as long as possible. When they peter out amongst the scree, trend left to reach firm rock at the base of an obvious tower. Ascend this on good holds and firm rock to gain the summit of Ill Crag.

The summit of Scafell Pike lies some 800m to the south west and is easily gained via the summit of Broad Crag and the well-trodden path that traverses the boulder field to the highest point in England.

To continue the traverse, descend south west from the summit cairn of Scafell Pike to gain Mickledore. Follow the crest of the ridge over the col until your way is barred by the rock of Scafell Crag. Drop down about 3m to the east from the top of Mickledore's crest to an obvious cleft. Climb this to gain the first platform, and traverse left to reach a short but slightly overhanging wall. The exposure now becomes only too apparent, so a rope should be employed as a fall would be very serious.

The holds are there, but are smooth and slope in the wrong direction for comfort. Although only 2.5m in height this wall demands a series of committing moves to gain the second platform.

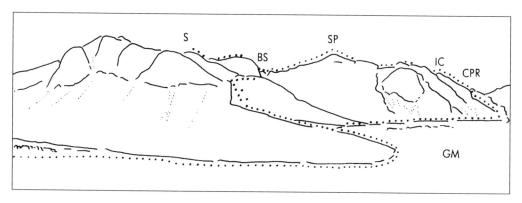

Scafell Traverse
SP – Scafell Pike; S – Scafell; GM – Great Moss; CPR – Cockly Pike Ridge; IC – Ill Crag;
BS – Broad Stand

Scafell Traverse – Mickledore and Broad Stand

M – Mickledore; BS – Broad Stand; FT – Foxes Tarn; S – Scafell

Beyond this a second, but easier wall provides access to the top of the Mickledore chimney. This is then crossed to provide access to a groove and then easier scrambling to the top of Scafell Crag and the summit.

If Broad Stand is out of condition, and it does tend to be greasy after rain, which makes the moves particularly difficult, then you can descend via the eastern flank of Mickledore to gain Foxes Tarn and a much easier, though roundabout approach to the summit of Scafell.

Descent: Retrace your steps north to the col between the summit of Scafell and Symonds Knot and drop south east down the path to Foxes Tarn. From here turn north east and descend via an obvious but steep and rocky path to the gully above Cam Spout. Stick to the north-east side of the waterfall and continue steeply down the well-marked but precipitous path to regain the Great Moss. There are paths on both sides of the River Esk, which can be difficult to ford, particularly if it is in spate, that lead back to Brotherikeld.

Central Fells

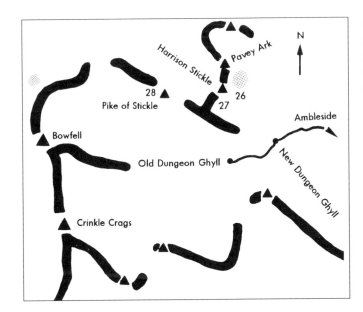

Route 26 – East Ridge of Harrison Stickle
Route 27 – South-East Ridge of Harrison Stickle
Route 28 – West Ridge of Pike of Stickle

Approaches: A593 from Ambleside via Skelwith Bridge and Elterwater. Rail link to Windermere. Limited bus service into Langdale from Windermere via Ambleside.

Accommodation: Camping – Langdale; youth hostels – Elterwater; B&B and hotels – Langdale and Elterwater.

Tourist information: 015394 32582.

Route 26

EAST RIDGE OF HARRISON STICKLE

Mountain: Harrison Stickle (736m)
Category: Scrambling and winter route
Grades: Scrambling – 2–3; climbing – Moderate; winter – II
Time: 4hrs
Distance: 4.5km

Height: 250m
Approach: GR 295 064; New Dungeon Ghyll Hotel
Route: GR 284 074
Maps: OS 1:25,000 Outdoor Leisure sheets 4 or 6; OS 1:50,000 Landranger sheets 89 or 90

Introduction: The valley of Langdale leads deep into the heart of the central core of the Lakeland fells. It is surrounded on all sides by steep and dramatic peaks, the most impressive clustered between Stickle Tarn and Pike of Stickle. They are collectively known as the Langdale Pikes; the highest is Harrison Stickle. Its East Ridge provides a fine mountaineering route directly from Stickle Tarn at its base to the summit.

In addition, this ridge can be readily combined with a descent via Jack's Rake, probably the most famous scram-

East Ridge of Harrison Stickle

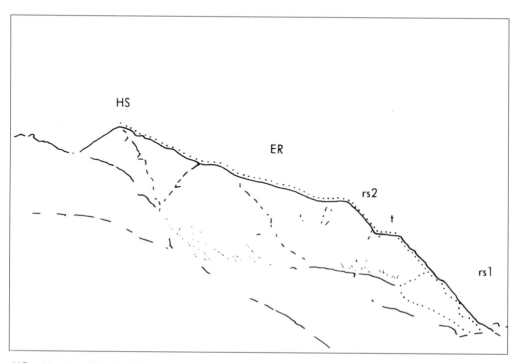

HS – Harrison Stickle; ER – East Ridge; rs1 – first rock step;t – terrace; rs2 – second rock step

ble in the Lake District. The Rake follows a bold rising/descending traverse across the magnificent south-east face of Pavey Ark. When combined they make for a fine expedition.

Situation: Harrison Stickle stands as an isolated peak when seen from the south and south east. To the west is the deep defile of upper Dungeon Ghyll; to the east, the prominent col that separates it from the great rock face of Pavey Ark. The East Ridge looks particularly spectacular when seen from the bottom of Stickle Ghyll, but its true character is best seen from the outflow of Stickle Tarn. From here it is seen as a raised series of steps on the skyline above.

Approach: From the New Dungeon Ghyll Hotel ascend the well-trodden path alongside Stickle Ghyll to the outflow from Stickle Tarn. A path goes along the south shore of the tarn for about 125m. It then ascends steeply to the base of some crags before traversing below them to a col. The rock band at the lowest point of the Crag is the start of the route.

Ascent: The first rock step is steep and the moves tricky; it is this pitch which demands that the route be graded 3. Trend left on compact holds to gain a grass terrace. Belays are not that apparent, so do not rely completely on slings; a selection of nuts will be needed. This step can, however, be avoided by walking around the base of the crag and traversing in from above the step.

Another rock step rears above the terrace, but the going is easier here and it can be taken directly. A series of easy-angled steps now provide pleasant scrambling on a broad ridge. The quality of the rock is remarkable and provides fine friction and sure holds.

Eventually a rising traverse along a gangway is reached. Move right to left along this, mostly on good holds but crossing an intimidating gap in the process. Once clear of the gangway the angle eases and a broken ridge providing a mixture of scrambling and walking leads to a broad summit.

Descent: From the summit descend to the north west to join up with the path that traverses the tops of the Langdale Pikes. The simplest way to return to the valley is to head initially south west, and then follow the path via Loft Crag and Mark Gate directly to the Dungeon Ghyll track.

A more adventurous option is to go north and then north west to the summit of Pavey Ark and descend via Jack's Rake. The Rake is an obvious feature that follows a rising traverse – in ascent right to left – across Pavey Ark. It is a grade 1 scramble and is very popular. The sense of exposure is, however, limited, for water has eroded a trough in the Rake and for most of the time it has its own natural 'safety barrier'.

In descent it is slightly more problematic, but still remains a grade 1 scramble. The major difficulty is finding the start. This is at the south-west corner of the summit plateau and is marked by an obvious cairn close by a dry stone wall. A second cairn is to be found on a rock step just below the edge of the plateau. The route is well trodden; be careful, however, not to dislodge any stones for there may be climbers on Pavey Ark's lower face.

Jack's Rake finishes at the scree at the base of Pavey Ark near Stickle Tarn. It is then simply a matter of following the edge of the tarn to pick up the outward route and return to the New Dungeon Ghyll Hotel.

Route 27

SOUTH-EAST RIDGE OF HARRISON STICKLE

Mountain: Harrison Stickle (736m)
Category: Scrambling and winter route
Grades: Scrambling – 1; climbing – N/A; winter – I
Time: 3–4hrs
Distance: 4km
Height: 110m
Approach: GR 295 064; New Dungeon Ghyll Hotel
Route: GR 283 073
Maps: OS 1:25,000 Outdoor Leisure sheets 4 or 6; OS 1:50,000 Landranger sheets 89 or 90

Introduction: This is a short and straightforward route that can easily be done if time is limited or on a winter's afternoon. Set amongst the Langdale Pikes, the setting is quite spectacular, the rock sound and for its grade both exposed and exciting.

Situation: The Langdale Pikes are one of the most spectacular parts of the Lake District. They soar over the deep trench of Langdale Valley and take on the appearance of isolated and interesting peaks. Appearances deceive and each of the Pikes has a gently sloping flank from the north.

Harrison Stickle is the highest of the Langdale Pikes and lies between the great crag of Pavey Ark and the huge pillar of Pike of Stickle. The South-East Ridge follows a fairly direct line up the South-East Flank rising above the deep gorge of Dungeon Ghyll.

Approach: Follow the path that heads westward from behind the Dungeon Ghyll and, when it splits after 300m, follow the branch that ascends the hillside towards Miller Crag and then turns below Pike Howe. The path then follows a rising traverse above Dungeon Ghyll. About 500m after clearing the base of Pike Howe, leave the path and climb directly up the fell-side to the base of the ridge.

Ascent: Locate a perched rock on a terrace below the ridge – there is a rock step directly behind this. Climb the rock step, which is quite steep for the grade, but the holds are good. After the step move left on the rock to some slabs that trend left. There are nodules on the slabs that provide sure holds.

The slab leads to the crest and this is followed directly over a series of rock steps. The crest continues directly in a straightforward manner almost to the summit of the ridge. This is terminated by the summit blocks, which are best taken off to the right. The summit of Harrison Stickle is but a short if rugged walk along the upper reaches of the main ridge.

Descent: Several paths dissect the summits of the Langdale Pikes and provide good walking on the open fells to the north of the pikes. This is, however, in direct contrast to the rugged grandeur to the south. The most direct descent is straightforward but the scenery is very spectacular.

Head north, then west and south from the summit of Harrison Stickle to pick up the path that cuts above the deep gorge of Harrison Stickle. This is a popular route, but is atmospheric nonetheless.

The South-East Ridge of Harrison Stickle

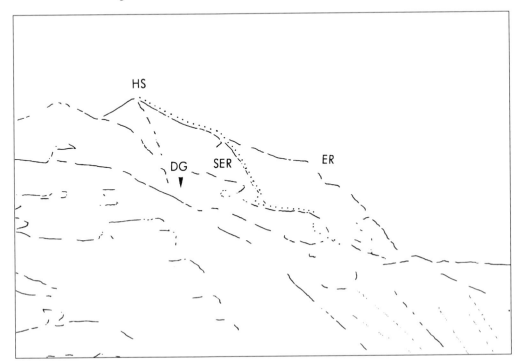

HS – Harrison Stickle; SE – South East Ridge; ER – East Ridge; DG – Dungeon Ghyll

Route 28

WEST RIDGE OF THE PIKE OF STICKLE

Mountain: Pike of Stickle (709m)
Category: Scrambling and winter route
Grades: Scrambling – 3; climbing – Easy; winter – II
Time: 5hrs
Distance: 7.5km
Height: 130m
Approach: GR 285 061; Old Dungeon Ghyll Hotel
Route: GR 272 073
Maps: OS 1:25,000 Outdoor Leisure sheet 6; OS 1:50,000 Landranger sheet 89 or 90

Introduction: Pike of Stickle is one of the Lake District's most striking peaks. When seen from Langdale it appears as a steep and imposing pyramid, dominating the head of the dale. While the rock on the south face does not lend itself to climbing, for the mountaineer the West Ridge provides a line that is both exposed and quite serious in nature. And despite a contrived approach, this is a fine route in a spectacular situation.

Situation: Pike of Stickle stands on the northern side of Langdale towards the head of the valley and is the most prominent feature in the dale. From the south it appears to be a free standing summit, but is in fact connected directly to a level plateau that stretches north beyond the Langdale Pikes.

The south face, known as Stickle Breast, is one of the most continuous steep slopes in the district, rising a vertical 600m in a horizontal 800m. Its base is surrounded by considerable scree slopes. To the east and the west it is defined by two major gullies.

On the western edge of Pike of Stickle is a narrow ridge and a series of pinnacles – this is the West Ridge. Its base is a grass platform which is well above the scree and can not be reached very easily directly from the valley floor. The platform can, however, be gained by dropping 60m down the gully that forms the western edge of Pike of Stickle, via the easy ground atop the northern slopes of Langdale on Martcrag Moor.

Approach: Go round the back of the Old Dungeon Ghyll Hotel and follow the very obvious track into Mickleden. After 1.5km a faint path can be seen zig-zagging up alongside Troughton Beck. Ascend this to Martcrag Moor and then cut back south east to gain the western edge of Pike of Stickle. Descend a short distance to find the top of the gully. Look down the gully: 60m below is the grass platform. Descend to this with care.

Ascent: From the grass platform, ascend a series of walls and ledges to the right of the ridge. When the way is blocked by a steep wall, head right into a grassy gully that leads to a slab that in turn provides access to the main crest.

A series of pinnacles now appear; traverse to the right and climb a crack. This leads to a second and larger pinnacle. The pinnacles provide good belays and should be used as such, for the next move is both testing and the situation exposed.

Go to the back of the pinnacle and ascend by a steep, fierce crack to gain easier ground on the terraces above. Ahead lies a steep wall with some slabs above. Avoid the wall to the right by way of the gully and then go left to get on to the slabs. An arête now rears up; ascend this for about 5m and then traverse right along a ledge to avoid a steep step. Above lies easier ground and a path to the summit.

Descent: From the top of the Pike of Stickle the most direct route to the valley is to descend via the rugged but well-worn path that descends over Loft Crag and Mark Gate to the New Dungeon Ghyll Hotel, and then go back to the start point along the valley road or the footpath that skirts below Raven Crag.

The West Ridge of Pike of Stickle

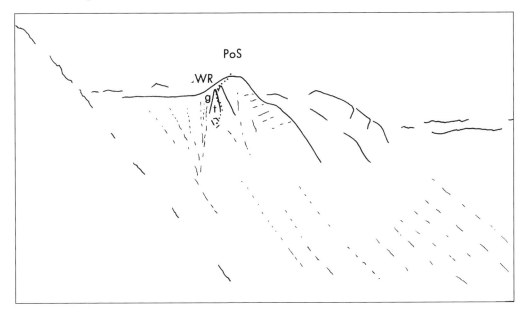

PoS – Pike of Stickle; WR – West Ridge; g – gully; t – terrace

Western Fells

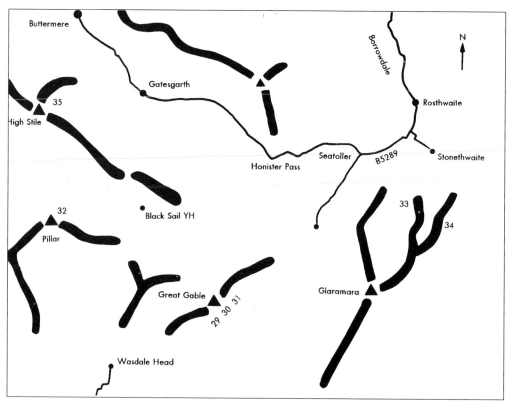

Route 29 – Needle Ridge
Route 31 – Sphinx Ridge
Route 33 – Intake Ridge
Route 35 – Chockstone Ridge

Route 30 – Arrowhead Ridge via Eagle's Nest Gully
Route 32 – The Old West Route of Pillar Rock
Route 34 – Cam Crags Ridge

Approaches: From Keswick, take the B5289 to upper Borrowdale, the Honister Pass to Buttermere, then to Ennerdale. From Ambleside, take the Wrynose/Hardknott Pass to Eskdale and on to Wasdale, or the A589 to Coniston, Torver and the Ulpha Fell road. Rail link to Windermere, bus to Keswick. Bus from Keswick to upper Borrowdale. Wasdale and Ennerdale have no bus link. Mountain Goat Bus from Keswick to Buttermere.

Accommodation: Camping – sites in Borrowdale, Seathwaite and Wasdale Head; youth hostels – Wasdale, Gillerthwaite, Black Sail, Buttermere, Longthwaite and Honister Hause; B&B and hotels – Buttermere, Wasdale, Rosthwaite, Stonethwaite, Seatoller and Cockermouth.

Tourist Information: 017687 77294 and 01900 822634.

Route 29

NEEDLE RIDGE

Mountain: Great Gable: (889m)
Category: Rock climb
Grades: Scrambling – N/A; climbing –
Very Difficult; winter – N/A
Time: 6hrs
Distance: 9.5km
Height: 280m
Approach: GR 187 088 – Wasdale Head
Route: GR 210 099
Maps: OS 1:25,000 Outdoor Leisure
sheets 4 or 6; OS 1:50,000 Landranger
sheets 89 or 90

Introduction: *It must be fully understood
that an ascent of Needle Ridge falls well outside the established realm of scrambling –
the term that describes most of the routes in
this book – since it is a full-blown mountaineering rock climb.* The use of a complete set of climbing gear and an 11mm
or double 9mm rope is required. The
route needs to be fully pitched and protected throughout. Having said all of
that, Needle Ridge is fairly straightforward by climbing standards, readily
climbed in mountain boots rather than
rock shoes, and is without doubt one of
the finest routes that can be styled an
'alpine' ridge in England and Wales.

The ridge is named after Napes
Needle, which is an isolated pinnacle
found at its base. Both were climbed by
W.P. Haskett-Smith: the ridge in 1884 –
the first climbing route on Gable – and
the Needle itself in 1886. Although
Haskett-Smith was probably blissfully
unaware of it at the time, these two
routes fall within two distinct eras of
mountaineering history and mark an
important watershed.

In climbing Napes Needle – which is
a relatively short but athletic exercise – it
was deemed that the climb was done for
itself. This was a departure from previous practice where the route was done
as an overhaul expedition to a summit
and after the style of mountaineering in
the Alps. Routes previously done in this
country were mainly regarded as a practice of techniques for alpine expeditions.

On this basis Napes Needle is generally regarded as the first 'rock climb'
and the birthplace of rock climbing as a
pursuit with its own identity. In a historical context, Needle Ridge pre-dates
this idea and has all the characteristics
of a mountaineering route.

Situation: Great Napes and its subsidiary neighbour, White Napes, form
the lower of two rock bands that girdle
Great Gable's south-west face. Directly
above and leading to Gable's summit
are the rocks of Westmorland Crag.
Together they form the well-known
pyramid that is associated with Great
Gables. Great Napes is bounded in the
east by the large gully known as Great
Hell Gate and in the west by Little Hell
Gate. Traversing around its base, but
above the significant scree slopes, is a
path known as the Gable or Climber's
Traverse. The face is dominated by four
major ridges.

Needle Ridge is the most easterly of
the Nape's four ridges. Looking directly
at Gable's south-west face it is found on
the eastern edge next to Tophet Wall,
rising directly above Napes Needle. It is
bounded to the west by Needle Gully.

Approach: From Wasdale Head, follow
the track that ascends alongside
Lingmell Beck, before turning off to join
the path that follows a rising traverse
below Gable's massive screes and on to
the col at Styhead Pass.

At Styhead pick up the path that
leads west-north-west between Kern
Knotts and Lower Kern Knotts. This is
the Gable Traverse and provides direct

access to the start of all the Napes Ridges. Follow this rugged path for 800m, crossing as you go the red screes of Great Hell Gate (where a spring is to be found) until the easily recognizable Napes Needle comes into view. Needle Ridge rises directly above Napes Needle.

Ascent: From the gap between the Needles, ascend the obvious slab. The holds are polished and the moves quite delicate, and can be difficult if wet. Aim for the chimney that trends to the left at the top of the slabs. Enter and climb this to a good belay stance at the bottom of a steep wall.

Although the wall is steep, the holds are good and after 5m the angle eases somewhat. Easier going is followed by a second but more broken wall which in turn leads to the next belay stance.

The ridge now starts to narrow to a well-defined crest but this still can not be gained directly. To do this, traverse to the left for 7m over easy ground and gain a pronounced rib. Climb this directly for 15m. It is exposed, so it is essential that it is properly protected; nevertheless the holds are apparent and sound. This leads to the crest of the ridge and a stupendous position.

Needle Ridge

Ascend the crest for about 10m until the way is barred by a rock step; this is turned to the right in a corner. Once out of the corner, the crest can be regained and ascended by a groove, but once again the way is barred, this time by an overhang. Traverse below this to the right until the obstacle is cleared and then ascend on good holds to regain the crest.

The overhang is the last major obstacle and ahead lies a fine gendarmed ridge at a more moderate angle; follow this for 35m. Only now is it possible to dispense with fixed belays and move roped together; nevertheless, slings should be placed over the many spikes as running belays as a sensible precaution. Needle Ridge tops out at a level and grassy neck that connects Napes with Great Gable.

Above is Westmorland Crag. While there is a 'walkers' route that avoids this and leads to Gable's summit, it is rather scrappy and hardly in tune with this expedition. A fine ridge does, however, ascend Westmorland Crag and leads to the summit.

To locate it, go to the base of the crag and pick up the faint path that traverses below the crags and across the scree. Follow this to the right until a square

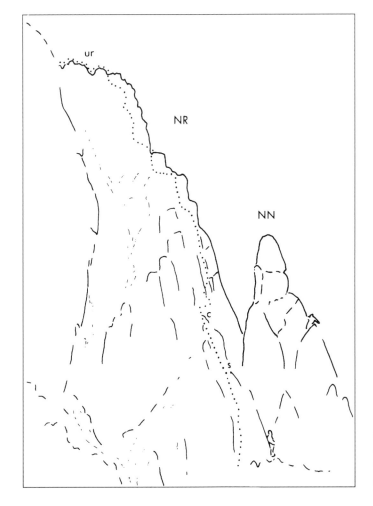

NR – Needle Ridge; NN – Napes Needle; s – slab; c – chimney; ur – upper ridge

topped and broken block is gained. At the right-hand edge of the block is a gully. From the gully ascend a corner to gain the crest of the ridge.

For the best sport, stick to the crest, which is easier than it looks and has good holds. The top of the ridge is marked by Westmorland Cairn; Gable's summit is but a short walk away.

Descent: There are a number of obvious and interesting paths off the top of Great Gable. Those to the south involve sustained and knee-jarring descents – if you intend to scree-run Little Hell's Gate be careful to pick the right gully.

One alternative which breaks up the descent and takes in more of this fine mountain is to go north east to Windy Gap and then drop down into Stone Cove. Traverse below the impressive Gable Crag, on to Beck Head and then pick up the path that leads to Wasdale Head.

Route 30

ARROWHEAD RIDGE VIA EAGLE'S·NEST GULLY

Mountain: Great Gable (899m)
Category: Scramble/rock climb and winter route
Grades: Scrambling – 2/3; climbing – Moderate; winter – III
Time: 5–6hrs
Distance: 9.5km
Height: 80m
Approach: GR 187 088; Wasdale Head
Route: GR 208 100
Maps: OS 1:25,000 Outdoor Leisure sheets 4 or 6; OS 1:50,000 Landranger sheets 89 or 90

Introduction: Arrowhead Ridge is named after a large and distinctive pillar midway up the ridge. If the entire ridge is climbed directly it is graded as a sustained Very Difficult rock climb and falls just outside the domain of this book. There is, however, a scrambling route which leaves out the difficulties at the start by ascending the neighbouring Eagle's Nest Gully to regain the ridge in its upper reaches.

Here the angle eases, but the crest remains quite sharp and very spectacular. A real sense of exposure is present, though it is never intimidating and the views on to the Nape's other ridges are superb.

Situation: Great Napes and the subsidiary White Napes form the lower of two rock bands that girdle Great Gable's south west face. Above the Napes is Westmorland Crag and together they form the well-known rock pyramid that can be seen from Wasdale. The outstanding feature of the Napes is a series of bold.and steep ridges.

Arrowhead Ridge is in the middle of Great Napes, to the west of the other central ridge, Eagle's Nest Ridge. The two are separated by Eagle's Nest Gully which provides an alternative and scrambling grade start to both of these ridges. Arrowhead Ridge ascends directly, the crest trending slightly left to right. The lower section is quite steep but this is avoided. Towards the top of the steep section is the arrowhead while, above, the upper section is relatively level but quite narrow.

Approach: From Wasdale Head, follow the track that ascends alongside Lingmell Beck, before turning off to join the path that follows a rising traverse below Gable's massive screes and on to the col at Styhead Pass.

At Styhead pick up the path that heads west-north-west between Kern Knotts and lower Kern Knotts. This is the Gable Traverse and provides direct access to the start of all of the Napes ridges. Follow this rugged path for about 800m, crossing as you go the red screes of Great Hell Gate (where a spring is to be found) until the famous Napes Needle comes into view. Hereabouts the path splits into two; follow the right-hand fork.

An interesting diversion and a scramble in its own right – known as 'threading the Needle' – is to be enjoyed by negotiating the gully and the gap between Napes Needle and the main crag.

Beyond Napes Needle, the going gets more rugged but the path is well marked. Below Eagle's Nest Ridge is a slab and a steep gully. This is Eagle's Nest Gully and the start of the route.

The base of Arrowhead ridge is on the left-hand side of the gully. The actual arrowhead can be identified at the top of the initial buttress.

Arrowhead Ridge via Eagle's Nest Gully

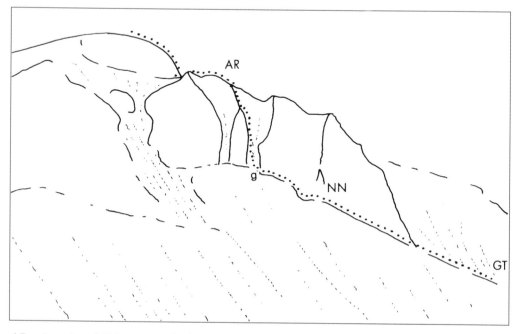

AR – Arrowhead Ridge; g – gully; NN – Napes Needle; GT – Gable Traverse

Ascent: To avoid the direct start, ascend the gully by the rocks on the left-hand side. A slight track can be seen; follow this to the base of a rock band that blocks the gully. To overcome this, ascend a slanting groove which trends left to right, then go back into the gully when the rocks and a chockstone are cleared.

Further up the gully, another section of steep rock can be avoided to the left, after which the ascent is over scree until the gully forks. Take the left branch to gain a grass shelf that sits on the crest of the ridge.

From here the ridge is relatively straightforward as the climbing pitches have been bypassed. Ascend a short broken wall and then on to a rib. Care should be taken with some loose boulders.

Above is a flat shelf, with a slab beyond and then on to a broken crest with a series of ribs beyond. This ends at a grass neck which connects Napes to Gable itself.

Above the grass neck lies Westmorland Crag. It is possible to join a 'walkers' path that now leads to the summit of Great Gable, but a fine ridge which ascends the crag provides an alternative more in keeping with the overall project.

Pick up a faint path that traverses across the scree below Westmorland Crag and go right until a square topped and broken block can be seen. This marks the base of the ridge. Go to the right flank of the ridge and gain the crest up a corner.

Stick to the crest, which is easier than it looks, and ascend directly. An easier alternative does however lie in the gully. The top of this ridge is marked by the Westmorland Cairn and the summit rocks are close by.

Descent: As for route 29.

Route 31

SPHINX RIDGE

Mountain: Great Gable (899m)
Category: Scrambling and winter route
Grades: Scrambling – 2; climbing – Easy
(Difficult if the start is taken directly);
winter – II
Time: 5–6hrs
Distance: 9.5km
Height: 140m
Approach: GR 187 088
Route: GR 208 100
Maps: OS 1:25,000 Outdoor Leisure
sheet 4 or 6; OS 1:50,000 Landranger
sheet 89 or 90

Introduction: Sphinx Ridge is the only
one of all the fine rock ridges to ascend
Great Napes that provides a continuous
ascent for the scrambler. It is a technically straightforward but continuous
and exhilarating route directly up the
south-west face of Great Gable. The surroundings include some of the most
spectacular rock scenery in Britain and
a high mountain atmosphere pervades
the situation.

Situation: Great Napes and the subsidiary White Napes form the lower of
the two rock bands that girdle Great
Gable's south-west face. Above the
Napes is Westmorland Crag and together they form the well-known shape of
the rock pyramid that is seen from
Wasdale. The outstanding feature of
Napes is a series of bold and steep
ridges.

Sphinx Ridge is the most westerly of
these and forms the edge of Great
Napes where it borders Little Hell Gate
– the massive gully that separates Great

Sphinx Ridge

Napes from its smaller neighbour, White Napes. It rises directly above the upper path – known as either the Gable or Climber's Traverse – that crosses the bottom of the crag. Its base is indicated by the very obvious Sphinx Rock, named for obvious reason after the Egyptian antiquity.

Once the ridge gains the top of Great Napes it converges with the other Napes ridges to form a level grassy neck which connects with Westmorland Crag directly above. A ridge line then continues up Westmorland Crag and provides a direct approach to the summit of Great Gable.

Approach: As route 30 up to Napes Needle.

Beyond Napes Needle the going becomes more rugged, but the path remains well marked. Below Eagle's

Nest Ridge a slab and a steep-sided gully have to be negotiated, after which the obvious profile of Sphinx Rock becomes apparent.

Ascent: Sphinx Rock provides a very obvious reference point at the base of the route. There is, however, a choice of starts. The first is graded as a Difficult rock climb and is found directly behind Sphinx Rock. It involves a direct ascent of a groove to a belay stance, beyond which is easy climbing off to the left.

The start for the scramble is found in the gully which forms the eastern edge of Sphinx Ridge. Ascend this for 6m before traversing left out of the gully and on to the crest of the ridge.

There is now a series of rugged pinnacles, negotiated by a winding route. Beyond is a pronounced gap which is crossed in turn with an exposed move.

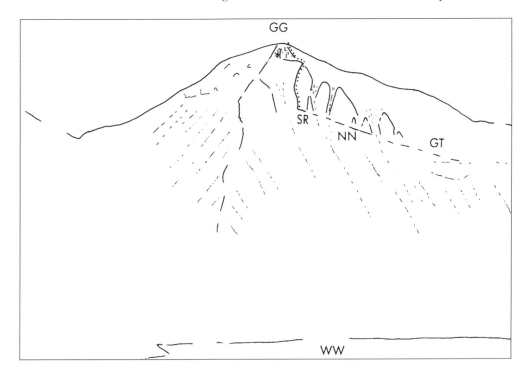

GG – Great Gable; SR – Sphinx Ridge; NN – Napes Needle; GT – Gable Traverse;
WW – Wast Water

A steepening of the ridge now occurs, but the crest can still be followed for 10m before a nasty rock step finally bars progress.

This can be avoided by traversing right along a gangway and back into the gully. The ridge proper can then be regained above the difficulties. The going now eases and the crest can be followed throughout until it merges with the main flank of the mountain. The views of the neighbouring Napes ridges are impressive.

Sphinx Ridge dwindles out atop Great Napes, where it merges with its neighbouring ridges to form a broad and grassy neck. The summit of Great Gable is, however, barred by West-morland Crag. While it is possible to join the 'walkers' path and avoid this rock band altogether, a fine ridge provides a more exhilarating alternative.

From the top of Great Napes pick up a faint path which traverses to the right across the scree to the base of an obvious ridge line, a square-topped and shattered block. Go below the block to the ridge's right-hand flank and gain the crest up a corner.

For the best sport, stick to the crest, which is easier than it looks and has good holds; it is, however, quite exposed and if it becomes too intimidating then the difficulties can be avoided by regaining the gully. The top of the ridge is marked by Westmorland Cairn; Gable's rocky summit is but a short walk away.

Descent: As for route 29.

Route 32

OLD WEST ROUTE OF PILLAR ROCK

Mountains: Pillar (892m) and Pillar Rock
Category: Scrambling and winter route
Grades: Scrambling – 3s; climbing – Moderate; winter – II/III
Time: 6–8+hrs
Distance: 16.5km
Height: 160m
Approach: GR 187 088; Wasdale Head
Alternative approach: GR 109 153; Bowness Knot
Route: GR 172 124
Overnight: GR 195 123; Black Sail Youth Hostel. *There is no vehicle access to the Hostel, nor is there a direct telephone link and it can only be reached after a long walk. It is closed in the winter (from the end of October to the end of March). Bed spaces are limited and should be booked by post well in advance.*
Maps: OS 1:25,000 Outdoor Leisure sheets 4 and 6 (4 gives nearly all the coverage required); OS 1:50,000 Landranger sheet 89

Introduction: Pillar Rock is without doubt the finest mountain feature in the Lake District. Its north face, seen from above the forestry plantations in Ennerdale, will leave an indelible impression. It is no exaggeration to say that Pillar appears to have all the stature of a classic alpine aiguille.

Pillar's north face has a serious air, for the rock is both compact and steep; consequently most of the routes to the summit of Pillar are technical rock-climbs. There is, however, one option that falls within the remit of this book and that is the original line up the face climbed in 1826 by a local man, John Atkinson, as a solo ascent. His route follows a rising traverse across the base of the upper face and then provides access up a fine and airy crest that reaches the summit directly.

Situation: Pillar Rock overlooks Ennerdale to the north – the most remote dale in the Lake District – while to the south is Wasdale. It should be noted that the roadhead for Ennerdale involves a long and circuitous drive and any approach from here involves a long walk along the forest track.

As a result the most practical approach is from Wasdale via Black Sail Pass. Even so, while it is feasible to do the approach, route and return in one day, it would be a long one. On this basis, it is worthwhile considering spending the night at Black Sail Youth Hostel.

Pillar Rock is named for its impressive phallic appearance, three of its four elevations presenting a prospect of uniform steepness. The fourth, its southern side, connects the rock to the main Pillar Massif by a narrow defile, Jordan's Gap, and the subsidiary summit of Phisgah. Although this flank is much shorter, it nevertheless presents a steep and intimidating prospect.

The topography of the rock is quite complex, and close inspection will show that the north side consists of not one, but two rock cones laid out in ascending order – known respectively as Low Man and High Man. Beyond High Mans and separated from it by Jordan's Gap and part of the main mountain, is another cone of rock known as Phisgah. Off to the east is another isolated pinnacle – detached from the main rock by Walker's Gully (not a walking approach) – called Shamrock.

To the east of Pillar lies a rock cirque called Pillar Cove, to the west a deep watercourse known as West Waterfall.

Old West Route of Pillar Rock

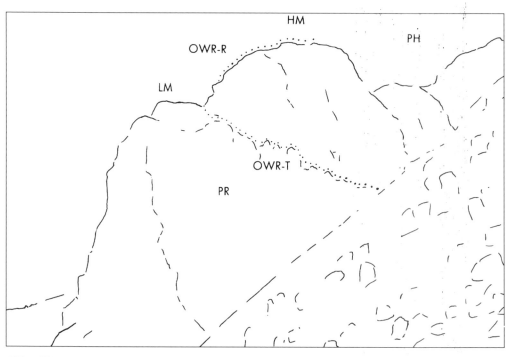

PR – Pillar Rock; LM – Low Man; HM – High Man; PH – Phisgah; WW – West Waterfall;
OWR-R – ridge; OWR-T – traverse

The whole crag is surrounded by impressive scree chutes and is situated high on the north flank of Pillar mountain.

Approach: This approach will enable the route to be done in one, albeit long, day. From Wasdale head pick up the path that heads north into Mosedale. When the path splits head north and then north east up Gatherstone Head to the summit of Black Sail Pass.

From here go west over Looking Stead (627m); 300m beyond the summit plateau the path splits by a small cairn and just below a significant steepening. Follow the right-hand branch – this path is known as the High Level Traverse (also called the Climber's Traverse). This follows an airy line above Pillar's spectacular northern flank.

Eventually the path reaches a col complete with large cairn, marked on the map as Robinson's Cairn; Pillar Rock will now be in full view. Continue along the traverse and go behind Shamrock and through the gap between Phisgah and Pillar Mountain. Descend via a gully down the western flank of High Man.

Be careful to avoid descending into the watercourse of West Waterfall and descend via the scree below Pillar's West Face. A faint path can be seen, descending into the cove below Pillar and providing access to the rising traverse of the Old West Route.

Alternative approach: It is very pleasant to approach via Ennerdale but this route is long, and getting to the roadhead is circuitous. It would need to be a very strong party who could start from here and hope to return in one day. On this basis consider overnighting at Black Sail Youth Hostel.

Leave the car park at Bowness Knot,

follow the track eastward alongside Ennerdale Water, past the youth hostel at High Gillerthwaite, and on through Ennerdale Forest to Black Sail Youth Hostel. Follow the track alongside Sail Beck to gain the summit of Black Sail Pass. Then follow the other approach.

Ascent: The rising traverse is obvious as it cuts left across the western flank of Pillar. Gain the ledge near a light-coloured patch of rock. Move across the ledge into a corner and back on to the ledge. Negotiate a second corner, this one capped by a large overhang, to reach another ledge barred by a rib.

Negotiate the rib to regain the ledge. Follow this until the way is barred by a slab. Cross the slab with care – this can be tricky if wet. After a gully is reached, ascend the right-hand edge for 8m until you can move left to gain a ledge complete with an obvious spike belay.

Easier ground now follows, and a level path leads to the crest which in turn provides access to the summit of Low Man. The main crest of the upper ridge is obvious, although gaining this is far from straightforward. From another good spike belay ascend some steepish rocks for 6m, then descend left via a slab to a small grass bay.

Ascend directly from the bay; a good belay exists up a rake and a small detour to make use of this is worth considering. Gain a platform after 6m and then traverse right to ascend some steep rock up to a perched block and then directly up a crack system. These moves are exposed and some of the holds appear dubious, so they demand a good belay. After this, easier ground leads to the summit of High Man.

Descent: The descent from High Man utilizes Slab and Notch (in reverse Notch and Slab). This is a grade 3

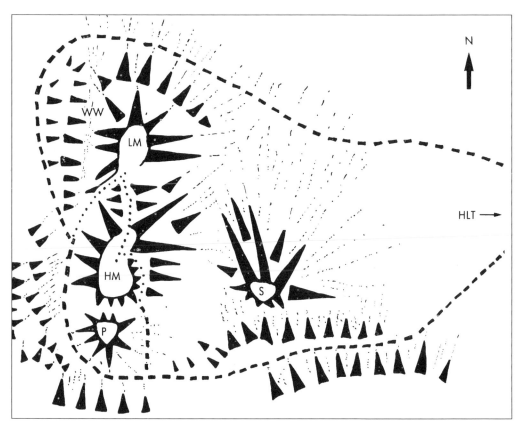

Approaching Pillar Rock. LM – Low Man; HM – High Man; P – Phisgah;
S – Shamrock; WW – West Waterfall; HLT – High Level Traverse

scramble in its own right and it is important that you do not relax at this stage. A belay is sensible.

This is reached via a gully off to the eastern side of High Man. Descend the gully until it widens, gain a slab, traverse this on good holds to a large flake, then descend steeply but on good holds to the notch. A good belay is necessary.

Descend to a second slab and tra-verse across this, descending first to its base before ascending its far edge to drop down steeply to the easier ground beyond. Follow the path below Phisgah to the gap between it and the main mountain. Return along the High Level Traverse and Black Sail Pass, and then on to Black Sail Youth Hostel or Wasdale Head.

Route 33

INTAKE RIDGE

Mountains: Rosthwaite Fell (612m) and Glaramara (783m)
Category: Scrambling route
Grades: Scrambling – 3; climbing – Moderate; winter – II
Time: 6hrs
Distance: 10.5km
Height: 180m
Approach: GR 251 137; Strands Bridge
Route: GR 253 128
Maps: OS 1:25,000 Outdoor Leisure sheet 4; OS 1:50,000 Landranger sheets 89 or 90

Introduction: Intake Ridge is probably the best known of all of Bentley Beetham's rock climbs/scrambles. It has to be said, however, that the route is not a continuous ridge, and also that it is far too close to the valley to maintain a high mountain atmosphere. Nevertheless, it provides superb scrambling and consists of a series of short but quite technical sections.

The name comes from the Lakeland term for the dry stone wall in a valley that separates, or 'takes in', the grazing pasture from the open fell-side.

Situation: Rosthwaite Fell is the northern end of a large ridge that extends from the core of the Lakeland Fells around Esk Hause. Cutting into the northern slopes of Rosthwaite Fell is the narrow defile of The Combe. At the entrance of The Combe and up the eastern side, Intake Ridge ascends as a series of outcrops from the screes above the valley floor.

Approach: Leave the B5289 by Strands Bridge and follow the track that crosses the bridge south for 100m before branching off left along the footpath that is signposted for The Combe. Follow this through the wood until it runs alongside Combe Ghyll.

A short distance after you emerge from the woods, a dry stone wall runs across the path. Go through the gate and then look immediately left up the steep hillside. The wall follows a line due east for 300m before turning north in an obvious right angle. The rocks of Intake Ridge rise directly above this corner.

Ascent: At the base of the first outcrop lies a large flake; ascend the crack on the left on good holds. Easy-angled rocks now lead to a grass platform. Move right for 7m to gain the next outcrop.

This takes the form of a rib and is steeper and more continuous than the first outcrop. Climb a steep wall to the left of a rock nose before going left again and up another steep wall, this time on large and well-spaced holds, before gaining a slab. When the slab steepens move left to gain a grass ledge.

Above the ledge rise some broken rocks and a steep wall. Ascend the rocks and then move right to avoid the wall, go round a corner on a narrow slab, and traverse into a large scoop in the rock.

Above the scoop lies the crux of the route; a large bulbous dome known as the glaciated slab lies above. There are two alternative ways to overcome it: both require a rope and belay. The first involves a ramp off to the right. The initial moves are straightforward, but get more difficult once you are committed. The ramp leads to the slab but the way is then barred by an awkward bulge. Trust to your feet and then a high step up left leads to easier but very exposed ground above.

The second alternative, which is the more difficult of the two, involves

Intake Ridge

climbing the crack at the back of the scoop. This is both steep and awkward. The crack leads in a rising traverse to the top of the slab.

Move left to a rock spur and head towards an obvious buttress off to the left, climb a vegetated gully, and then move left to easier ground. Steep rocks now bar further progress; to avoid them go off to the right along a terrace until you reach an edge. From here climb steeply to the left of a nose of rock to gain a ledge. Beyond is a slab which can

be ascended in a rising traverse to the right and leads to easier ground and the top of the ridge.

Descent: The subsidiary summit of Bessyboot lies just to the south east, but in common with the rest of Rosthwaite Fell the ground is broken and complex. A tarn lies due south of Bessyboot and the approach is marked by a series of cairns. From the tarn head south and then south west for 1.75km to the summit of Glaramara.

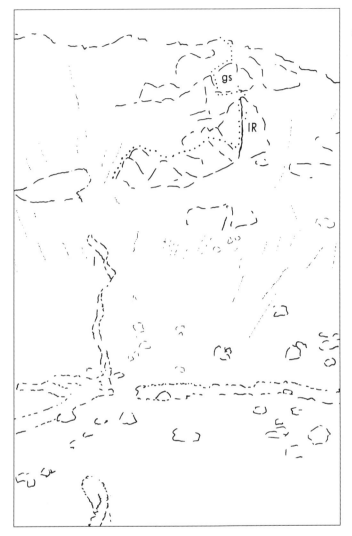

IR – Intake Ridge; I – Intake;
gs – glacial slab

From here the most direct descent to the valley is to descend steeply north west along the path down Hind Gill to Seathwaite. A more convenient descent to regain the start point and avoid a long road walk, however, is to head north and then north-north-east over Thornthwaite and drop down into The Combe to regain the outward path.

Route 34

CAM CRAGS RIDGE

Mountain: Glaramara (783m)
Category: Scrambling and winter route
Grades: Scrambling – 2; climbing –
Moderate; winter – II
Time: 5hrs
Distance: 11km
Height: 220m
Approach: GR 262 137; Stonethwaite
Route: GR 262 110
Maps: OS 1:25,000 Outdoor Leisure
sheet 4; OS 1:50,000 Landranger sheet
89 or 90

Introduction: Cam Crags Ridge follows
a direct and impressive line from
the floor of Langstrath to the top of the
Glaramara massif. At first glance the
ridge looks intimidating and steep, but
the going is actually relatively straightforward with good holds and few technical difficulties – all of which can be
avoided. The route was one of many
lower-grade rock climbs established by
Everest veteran Bentley Beetham in and
around Borrowdale in the mid-1930s. It
is now rightly regarded as a classic
Lakeland scramble.

Situation: Glaramara extends as a
major spur from the high ground that
forms the central core of the Lakeland
Fells to the head of Borrowdale. It consists of a broad but rocky and broken
ridge defined in the west by Seathwaite
and in the east by Langstrath.

Cam Crags Ridge is found on
Glaramara's eastern flank overlooking
Langstrath. The ridge is flanked by
Woof Gill to the south and a series of
smaller gullies to the north. From below
its base, the line is obvious and well
defined, rising as a chain of rock from
the supporting slopes.

Approach: From Stonethwaite pick up
the path that leads via the campsite and
past the waterfalls at Galley Force, turning due south at the junction of
Langstrath Beck and Greenup Gill into
Langstrath. From the stream junction
follow the path on the west side of the
beck for almost 2km. Cam Crag ridge
should be apparent on the skyline.
When you are directly below its base
ascend the slopes to a small levelling at
Woof Stones.

Ascent: An obvious rock step can be
seen above a series of boulders – gain
this by a traversing line. Ascend the wall
to the left and then climb a small arête to
gain the broad crest of the ridge. Once on
the ridge there are numerous lines that
can be followed – mostly on excellent
holds – but the best sport is to be had off
to the right. If the going becomes too difficult then easier options exist by moving back to a series of grassy terraces on
the left.

The main crest of the ridge is broken
by a series of steep walls followed by
grassy terraces. The key to overcoming
the steps is up a line of cracks that follow
a rising traverse up the face of the ridge.
The first one does present a particular
problem, as it steepens into a pronounced corner. This is, however, overcome by a set of fine and obvious holds.
The going eases with height, but care
must be taken on the final step as the
rock is loose and the holds are far from
obvious.

Descent: The route gains Glaramara's
main ridge well to the north east of the
summit. This is 1km away and although
the ground is fairly level the going –
across boggy depressions and small
crags – is far from straightforward.
There is, however, a safe, direct descent
to Langstrath. From Glaramara summit

pick up the well-trodden path via Thorneythwaite Fell and descend via Combe Gill to upper Borrowdale and a 1km road walk to Stonethwaite.

Cam Crags Ridge

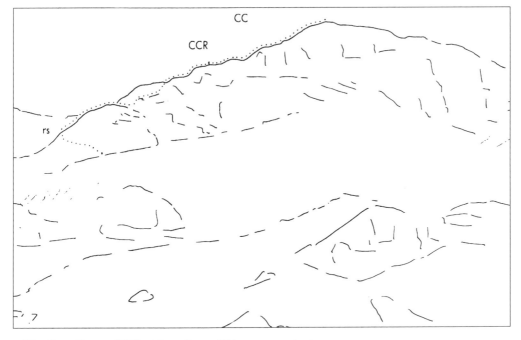

CC – Cam Crags; CCR – Cam Crags Ridge; rs – rock step

Route 35

CHOCKSTONE RIDGE

Mountain: High Stile (807m)
Category: Rock climb/scramble and winter route
Grades: Scrambling – 3s; climbing – Difficult; winter – III.
Time: 5hrs

Distance: 7.5km
Height: 200m
Approach: GR 193 150; Gatesgarth
Route: GR 172 147
Maps: OS 1:25,000 Outdoor Leisure sheet 4; OS 1:50,000 Landranger sheet 89

Introduction: High Stile ridge and its northern combes provide one of the

Chockstone Ridge

finest panoramas in the Lake District. Directly below High Stiles summit in Burtness Combe is Chockstone Ridge; when combined with the connected feature of Harrow Buttress it provides a direct ascent from the combe floor to the summit. The going is quite technical and sustained.

Situation: High Stile is the highest point on a ridge that trends north west-south east and overlooks Buttermere from the south. A series of hanging valleys, known locally as combes, have been scoured out of the northern flank. The largest is Burtness Combe and its headwall consists of a series of some of the largest crags in the district. Off to the north is the smaller face, known as Grey Crag. This route ascends the three

HS – High Stile;
HB – Harrow Buttress;
CR – Chockstone Ridge;
g – gully;
ut – upper tier

stacked tiers that make this crag.

The lower one is called Harrow Buttress and is graded as a difficult rock climb. The second, and dominant, tier is Chockstone Ridge, easier than the buttress and taking the form of a narrow ridge, which consists of a series of ascending towers and pinnacles. The whole route is topped by a broken buttress.

Approach: From Gatesgarth, head south west along the path that crosses the pasture at the western end of the lake. Where the fell starts to rise abruptly above the valley floor, pick up a fainter path that trends west below Low Crag until Comb Beck is reached. Follow the watercourse into the combe.

Look to the back of the combe and then swing to the north. Grey Crag is the southern flank of the spur that protrudes to form High Stile. The ridge rises above a fan of scree.

Ascent: From the base of Harrow Buttress, go right and ascend the side of the rib for a short distance to gain a ledge that will provide access to a chimney. Traverse into the chimney, climb this for about 7m, and then move left. Continue climbing until the way is barred by an overhang; traverse left. Above the overhang the going eases and a straightforward scramble leads to the top of Harrow Buttress.

Some broken rock leads to a traverse into a gully; Chockstone Ridge forms the other side of the gully. Drop into the gully and traverse down to the base of an obvious rock pillar. Ascend the ridge directly over a set of rock steps. The line is defined by the gully to the left and an obvious crack to the right.

This section comes to an end at the base of a rock pillar; traverse right into the gully to avoid this and then climb back behind the pillar to regain the crest.

If you have not yet belayed then this is the place to do so. Off to the right is a chimney, in itself relatively straightforward, but its exit is awkward and exposed. The chimney can also be avoided by traversing back into the gully.

The exit from the chimney provides the crux; above is a grassy shoulder and much easier going. The last obstacle barring the way to the summit of the stile is the final tier of rocks. This is, however, easily overcome through an obvious notch in the rock. The summit of High Stile is reached over the broad summit plateau.

Descent: The fastest way back to the valley is north west via Red Pike and The Saddle to Bleaberry Tarn. From here a path runs alongside Sourmilk Gill to the western end of Buttermere. This is, however, steep and unremitting. It is far more enjoyable to follow High Stile's main ridge over the seat and then down to the col at the top of Scarth Gap Pass, which can then be descended to Gatesgarth.

Eastern Fells

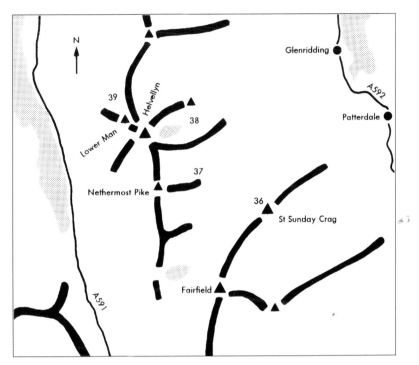

Approaches: A592 to Patterdale and Grasmere and A591 to Thirlmere. Bus link from Penrith and Ambleside/ Windermere to Glenridding and Patterdale. Kendal–Keswick bus drops off at Thirlmere.

Accommodation: Camping – Patterdale, Glenridding and Thirlmere; youth hostels – Patterdale, Helvellyn (Greenside) and Thirlmere; B & Bs and Hotels – Glenridding and Patterdale.

Tourist information: 015394 05245.

Route 36

PINNACLE RIDGE OF ST SUNDAY CRAG

Mountain: St Sunday Crag (841m)

Category: Scrambling and winter route
Grades: Scrambling – 3; rock climbing – Easy/Moderate; Winter – II
Time: 4–5hrs
Distance: 7.5km
Height: 180m
Approach: GR 390 161; Grisedale Bridge
Route: GR 367 140
Maps: OS 1:25,000 Outdoor Leisure sheet 5; OS 1:50,000 Landranger sheet 90

Introduction: The north-west flank of St Sunday Crag (the name applies to both the mountain and the rock face) dominates the impressive valley of Grisedale. Given its apparent steepness and its northern orientation it can appear a hostile and forbidding place. There is, however, tucked away in this vast curtain of rock a classic scramble of great

The Pinnacle Ridge of St Sunday Crag

PR – Pinnacle Ridge; SSC – St Sunday Crag; G – Grisedale

quality set amongst some of the Lake District's finest mountain scenery. For Pinnacle Ridge is one of the best – if not the best – upper-grade scramble in the Lake District.

Situation: Set well off to one side from the central portion of St Sunday Crag, Pinnacle Ridge follows a direct and steep line that leads to the summit area. The ridge is formed by a large gully that lies to the right and the open face of the crag on the left. Parts of the ridge are very exposed and narrow, particularly where it forms into a pinnacled arête at the top.

Approach: From Patterdale head up the lane that joins the A592 by Grisedale Bridge and follow this for 750m. Go through the gate and on through the paddock along the track. Continue past the point where another path leads up to the Brownend Plantation and head into Grisedale. Then follow the obvious track to Elmhow.

From the western edge of the Elmhow Plantation, pick up the path that zig-zags up to Blind Cove, until an obvious grass terrace is gained. Contour across the hillside on the terrace and a path below the scree slopes for about 500m until the base of a large scree fan is reached.

The base of the ridge consists of a jumble of blocks that rise above the scree. A large cannon-like block and a rowan tree further up the ridge will confirm your location. Do not be misled by an obvious pinnacle on the skyline further down the crag.

Ascent: Ascend the scree fan and then gain the blocks near a small cairn.

Scramble over the blocks until a defined edge emerges, which leads to the gun-like projection. Negotiate a slabby prow by trending to the right behind its smooth upper section.

The ridge continues over broken ground to the bottom of a large pinnacle, which can be avoided by going left and then striking for a groove that cuts up a steep wall. This is an exposed position but it can be easily belayed.

Ascend the groove directly on good holds, clear its top by stepping left, before returning to the steepening crest off to the right. An obvious step up a slab provides access to the airy crux of the pinnacled arête.

Exposed moves over a narrow crest (which should be belayed) provide a superb situation for, and great climax to, a classic route. The crest ends at a slab, which should be negotiated to the left, before descending another slab that leads to a neck of rock that connects the ridge to the mountain. Some easy ground follows before the rock again steepens. Head left to a series of rock steps that provide access to the summit area. The top of St Sunday Crag is marked by two cairns.

Descent: The most direct way back to the valley is to follow the path that heads north east and drop down to Gavel Moss and then over Birks (622m), before finally dropping down to Grisedale over Thornhow End.

Another possibility is to descend south west to Deepdale Hause. This provides access to either the Fairfield Horseshoe or the head of Grisedale and the great eastern corries of the Helvellyn range.

Route 37

NETHERMOST PIKE'S EASTERN RIDGE VIA EAGLE CRAG

Mountain: Nethermost Pike (891m)
Category: Scrambling and winter route
Grades: Scrambling – 2; climbing – Easy; winter – I
Time: 5–6hrs
Distance: 12km
Height: 390m
Approach: GR 390 161; Grisedale Bridge
Route: GR 356 143
Maps: OS 1:25,000 Outdoor Leisure sheet 5; OS 1:50,000 Landranger sheet 90.

Introduction: The eastern flank of the Helvellyn range contains a series of large cirques and fine ridges. So much attention is focused on the classic traverse of Striding and Swirral Edges, however, that the neighbouring ridges are often deserted. This ridge runs parallel to Striding Edge and leads directly to the summit of Helvellyn's immediate neighbour, Nethermost Pike.

Although Nethermost Pike's Eastern Ridge does not maintain the uniform sharpness of Striding Edge, it does narrow to a sharp and pinnacled arête in its upper reaches. The major technical difficulties which justify the grade are to be found on the approach to the crest of the ridge via a full-blown scramble up the ridge's southern flank on Eagle Crag.

Situation: Nethermost Pike is a major summit on the long ridge that forms the Helvellyn range. It lies 1km to the south of Helvellyn. In common with the rest of the range the mountain's eastern flank is deeply indented with deep corries divided by major ridges. The east-ern ridge is formed by Nethermost Cove to the north and by Ruthwaite Cove to the south.

Approach: From Patterdale leave the A591 by Grisedale Bridge and follow the narrow lane south west towards Grisedale Beck. Cross the beck by the bridge and follow the path as it rises towards Brownend Plantation. Follow the path westwards until it splits, when the lower route should be followed.

This leads for 3km into Grisedale, beyond Broomhill Plantation, until a faint path is gained that crosses over towards Nethermost Beck and the entrance to Nethermost Cove. Follow this path to some ruined mine buildings and the base of Eagle Crag.

Ascent: From the mine buildings a series of scree slopes ascend to the crag. In the centre of the crag is an obvious gully; this route takes a line on the right of the gully. Ascend the scree alongside a stone wall to gain the gully. Look for a pronounced nose of rock near another ruined building.

Climb the rock nose and then traverse towards the gully to gain some steep slabs. Climb these to a grass ledge. A series of short rock steps broken by grass ledges now appear. They present no major difficulties and can be ascended with ease. A rowan tree will eventually appear in the gully – head towards this and identify a large detached flake off to the right.

Gain the flake up some slabs, a series of moves which are delicate and should not be underestimated. Ascend on good holds behind the flake and on to a grass ledge.

From this ledge rises a rock rib; its ascent is exposed but provides a highlight of the route. Step right on and up the rib to gain another ledge. The way

Nethermost Pike's Eastern Ridge Via Eagle Crag

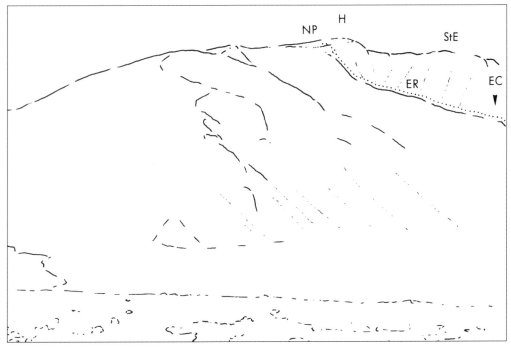

NP – Nethermost Pike; ER – Eastern Ridge; EC – Eagle Crag; H – Helvellyn;
StE – Striding Edge

in is now apparently barred by a steep wall. The key to overcoming this involves identifying the largest of a series of pinnacles that litter its base.

Go to the largest pinnacle and then cut round its back from the right to find a groove behind. Climb up the groove to gain another series of grass ledges which return the route to the edge of the gully. Easier scrambling now takes you to the crest of the ridge.

Once on the crest the going is straightforward, in summer little more than a rough walk. In winter, however, it is a stiffer challenge that is well within the frame of mountaineering. The route steepens and narrows as it gains the main ridge of the Helvellyn Range.

Descent: The summit of Helvellyn lies 1km to the north and is reached by skirting the top of the very impressive cirque of Nethermost Cove. The going is straightforward but look out for cornices in winter.

From Helvellyn's summit a number of descents are possible, but without doubt the most exciting is to reverse the traditional route over Striding Edge. Take care on the descent from the plateau on to the edge. The route is far from obvious from above and the descent is a lot steeper than it first appears. In winter, negotiating the massive cornice that forms at the top of the headwall can be problematic and the avalanche risk should be considered.

From the col where Striding Edge joins the main ridge a rock step will have to be ascended. If anything it is more fun this way round. Climb up the chimney and then continue along the edge to Hole-in-the-Wall and the well-trodden path that descends to Grisedale.

Route 38

HELVELLYN TRAVERSE

Striding and Swirrall Edges

Mountain: Helvellyn (950m)
Category: Scrambling and winter route
Grades: Scrambling – 1; climbing – N/A; winter – I
Time: 5hrs
Distance: 11km
Height: 240m
Approach: GR 387 169; Glenridding car park
Route: GR 358 153
Maps: OS 1:25,000 Outdoor Leisure sheet 5; OS 1:50,000 Landranger sheet 90

Introduction: The traverse of Striding Edge and Swirral Edge is rightly regarded as a classic. Straightforward in nature, it is for many people their first (and often only) mountaineering expedition. It is the most popular trip in the Lake District and conceivably the most trodden route of any mountain on the planet! It is definitely a place to be avoided on a Bank Holiday afternoon. Nevertheless under winter conditions it takes on an alpine aura – the mountain does hold snow longer than most in the Lakes – and becomes the domain of the mountaineer rather than the tourist.

Situation: Helvellyn's eastern flank consists of a series of deep corries and rocky ridges, of which Striding Edge and Swirral Edge are the most spectacular. They both buttress the summit plateau and are separated by Red Tarn and Helvellyn's great northern face. Swirral's other flank is formed by Brown Cove, Striding Edge's by the immense but gloomy Nethermost Cove. Striding Edge stretches for almost

1km; fairly level and of continuous rock for most of its length, it becomes turreted as it joins Helvellyn's craggy shoulder. Swirral Edge in contrast is a short, broken arête that falls away quickly to a col that connects Helvellyn to its shapely outlier, Catstycam. The traditional direction for the traverse is to ascend Helvellyn via Striding Edge and descend by Swirral.

Approach: There are a number of approaches to Helvellyn from the eastern side; this route minimizes the time spent on the road and leads directly to Striding Edge. From the car park/bus stop in Glenridding, cross the bridge and follow the lane along the south bank of the beck, until after 400m you pick up the path that leads to Westside and Lanty's Tarn. From the tarn descend to Brownend Plantation where you will strike the path that traverses above Grisedale and leads directly to the stile at Hole-in-the-Wall.

Traverse: From Hole-in-the-Wall the ridge line of Bleaberry Crags and then Striding Edge become apparent. Simply follow the well-trodden path until the crest narrows to an identifiable edge.

From here you get a good view of the ridge and the five rock outcrops which make up the edge will be identifiable. The first section is initially level, but soon narrows and this sets the going for most of the way. The narrow crest is easily followed although the exposure is noticeable. There is an easy path off to the flank, which switches from side to side. Half way along Striding Edge and overlooking Nethermost Cove is the first of Helvellyn's memorials: this one commemorates the fatal plunge of a huntsman.

At the fourth of the five outcrops the character of the route changes. Seen

Helvellyn Traverse

from a flank this is the most noticeable feature on the ridge and takes the form of a tower. On the edge you will notice a broadening of the crest, which is then followed by a 7m scramble down a chimney to a pronounced col. This is the trickiest point on the ridge, but is soon overcome.

Beyond the col there is a smaller tower and col to negotiate, then Striding Edge merges with its mountain and Helvellyn's summit slopes rear impressively upwards. Numerous paths dissect the broken crags, but trend left to avoid being forced on to Helvellyn's northern face. A steep and at times loose scramble of about a 50m will soon bring you to the summit plateau.

Once on the plateau the character of the mountain changes completely and opens out in all directions. The summit area is dominated by a shelter and a trig point, however, the highest point is only marked by a modest cairn. Off the sum-

mit, 10m down the western flank, a small stone block commemorates the first safe landing of an aircraft on a British mountain.

Descent: Locating the top of Swirral Edge prior to descent can be problematical as it is hidden from view below a convex slope. It lies 100m to the north west of the trig point and can be reached by following the path that skirts the edge of the plateau atop Helvellyn's steep northern face. In winter be careful of the cornices that form here.

A small cairn marks the spot to start the descent; from here turn north eastward down the slope until the rocks of the ridge appear. The way then becomes apparent and well marked with scratches on the rock. There are several paths through the broken ground on either flank, but the best scrambling is to be had by sticking to the crest itself until the col below Catstycam is reached. A

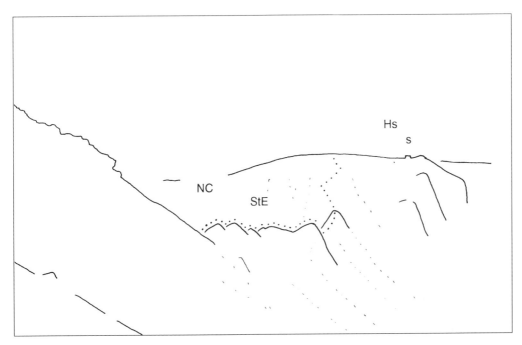

StE – Striding Edge; Hs – Helvellyn summit; NC – Nethermost Cove; s – shelter

path down to Red Tarn then becomes apparent.

From Red Tarn you can return via Hole-in-the-Wall, either into Grisedale or via the wall along the top of Birkhouse Moor, then descending into Little Cove and Rattlebeck Bridge. For a quicker descent, head down alongside Red Tarn Beck to Greenside and then follow the track down Glenridding.

Route 39

STEPPED RIDGE

Mountain: Lower Man (925m) and Helvellyn (949m)
Category: Scrambling and winter route
Grades: Scrambling – 2: climbing – Easy; winter – I/II
Time: 4–5hrs
Distance: 7.5km
Height: 170m
Approach: GR 316 169; Swirls car park
Route: GR 331 161
Maps: OS 1:25,000 Outdoor Leisure sheet 5; OS 1:50,000 Landranger sheet 90

Introduction: In contrast to Helvellyn's complex and spectacular eastern slopes, the western flank appears at first glance to have little to offer by way of ridge routes. While there are many excellent ghyll scrambles on this side, glaciation or frost-thaw shattering – the two architects of ridges and cirques – has had little effect hereabouts. The one area that does, however, provide potential is Brown Cove Crags.

Stepped Ridge ascends the western edge of these crags and enables height to be gained quickly and in a challenging manner. The line follows an easy-angled and quite broad ridge broken up into a series of steps. The difficulties are in keeping with its grade and the rough grey rock is a delight to scramble on.

Situation: Helvellyn Gill tumbles down the steep slopes of the mountain's western flank. Brown Cove Crags loom over the upper reaches of the deep valley that the water has carved out below the summit of Lower Man. It is important not to confuse the crags with Brown Cove, a small cirque found on the other side of the main Helvellyn ridge.

Stepped Ridge follows the crest at the western edge of the crags.

Approach: The most direct approach follows a steep path from the car park and picnic area overlooking Thirlmere on the A591 and ascends alongside Helvellyn Gill to a point directly below the ridge.

Ascent: From the path, identify the western edge of the crag and ascend the scree slope to reach it. The base of the ridge is blocked by a steep rock step. This can be avoided by moving right to gain a rock terrace that follows a rising traverse to provide access to the main crest of the ridge.

Stick to the left of the ridge and ascend a grass ledge and a small rock step. Atop the step is a rib which is itself topped by a block. Climb the rib and then squeeze through the gap below the block, after first removing your ruck-sack.

Above the block the ridge consists of a series of blocks – some of which are loose and demand care – and slabs. Move left at first, but go right to negotiate the slab, before moving back left to regain the crest. The next series of moves is exposed and demands care, though fortunately the rock provides superb friction and is sound.

Ascend to a platform and then up the edge to gain easier ground above. The ridge then narrows, but is in turn blocked by a rock step. Move left and then step down to gain a series of flakes; climb these directly, but delicately, to regain the crest. Next comes a series of ledges, best climbed on the left.

After a section of easier ground, the ridge is once again blocked by a slab, so move right and then left to regain the ridge. Yet another slab bars the way but this can be ascended to the left, gaining

Stepped Ridge

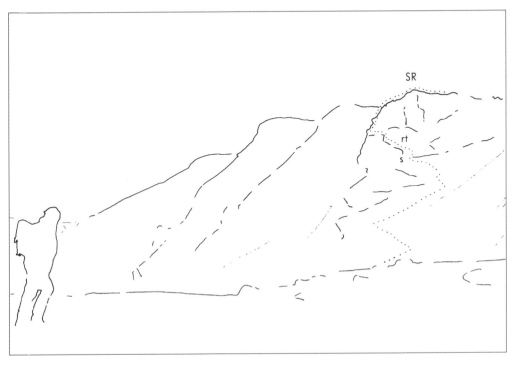

SR – Stepped Ridge; s – slab; rt – rock terrace

a ledge to the side of the ridge. Ascend a series of flakes, some of which are loose, then from atop the final flake regain the crest. This series of moves is over some loose rock, is often delicate and is continuously exposed. It should thus be belayed.

All that now remains is a short arête which is barred by a balanced block. Go under the block and ascend the left side of the arête to gain the top of the ridge and the summit ridge of Lower Man.

Descent: You are now atop the main Helvellyn ridge and have access to the largest area of continuous high ground in the Lake District. Any number of fell-walking options are now possible and Helvellyn summit is 750m to the south east.

The most direct descent back to the start point but avoiding the outward route is to use the old pony track. Go due north from the summit of Lower Man over White Side and descend alongside Brund Gill to the waterfalls of Fisherplace Gill, where the path turns south and south east to descend to Thirlspot and a 750m road walk to return to the car park.

North-Western Fells

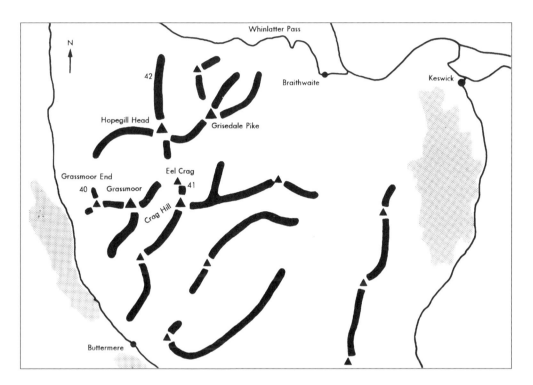

Route 40 – *Grassmoor's North-West Arête*
Route 41 – *Tower Ridge*
Route 42 – *North Ridge of Hopegill Head*

Approaches: From Keswick, A66 and then B5292 over Whinlatter Pass or Borrowdale and the B5289 over Honister Pass. Limited Mountain Goat Bus service to Buttermere.

Accommodation: Camping – Buttermere and Braithwaite; youth hostels – Buttermere, Gatesgarth and Keswick; B&B and hotels – Buttermere, Braithwaite and Keswick.

Tourist information: 017687 72803.

Route 40

GRASSMOOR'S NORTH-WEST ARETE

Mountain: Grassmoor (852m)
Category: Scrambling and winter route
Grades: Scrambling – 1 (just); climbing – N/A; winter – I
Time: 4hrs
Distance: 7.5km
Height: 250m
Approach: GR 159 209; car park at Lanthwaite Green

Grassmoor's North-West Arête

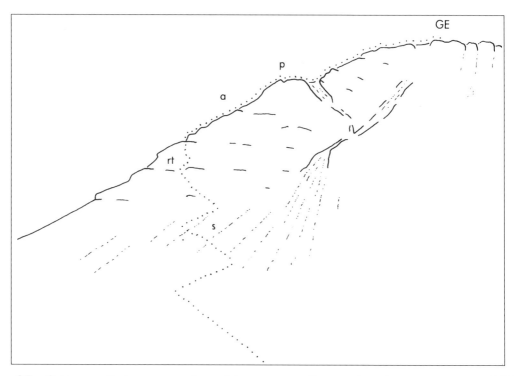

GE – Grassmoor End; s – scree; rt – rock terrace; a – arête; p – pinnacle

Route: GR 165 207
Maps: OS 1:25,000 Outdoor Leisure sheet 4; OS 1:50,000 Landranger sheet 89

Introduction: The craggy west face of Grasmoor – often referred to as Grasmoor End – looms over Crummock Water in a most impressive and intimidating manner. Famed for the winter climbing found in its gullies, its north-west edge is, however, a fairly continuous rock ridge. An ascent of this is very straightforward and can only just be described as a scramble, but the situation is magnificent and one to savour.

Situation: Grassmoor End rears up directly from the valley in the form of a dark pyramid. It was created by the glaciers that flowed down the dale; they ground down the western end of Grassmoor creating a classic truncated spur. The north-west arête follows the left-hand edge of the crag.

Approach: The arête is in full view of the car park at Lanthwaite Green. Simply follow the path that heads eastward towards Gasgale Gill, branch off right up the hillside after 250m and go straight up the hillside. A tongue of light-coloured scree acts as a useful aiming point.

Ascent: Go to the left of the lowest point of the crag and head for a break in the rock that provides access to a rising traverse up a rake of rock. Traverse up this to the right to an obvious terrace.

Above and to the left is an arête topped by a fine rock pinnacle. Climb the arête directly to the pinnacle. The pinnacle marks the end of the scramble, but there is still some rugged walking around the top of Grassmoor End crags to gain the summit. This takes the form of a rugged curving ridge. Grassmoor's actual summit lies 700m to the east of the top of Grassmoor End.

Descent: The simplest way back to Lanthwaite Green is to traverse over Grassmoor, descend to Coledale Hause and then descend via Gasgale Gill to the start point. From Coledale Hause it is, however, a simple matter to reach Tower Ridge on Eel Crag (see Route 41: Tower Ridge) and Hopegill Head (see Route 42: The North Ridge of Hopegill Head).

Route 41

TOWER RIDGE

Mountain: Crag Hill (839m)
Category: Scrambling and winter route
Grades: Scrambling – 1; climbing – N/A; winter – I
Time: 5–6 hrs
Distance: 10km
Height: 200m
Approach: GR 227 236; car park
Route: GR 194 208
Maps: OS 1:25,000 Outdoor Leisure sheet 4; OS 1:50,000 Landranger sheet 89

Introduction: There is no mention of Tower Ridge on the OS map and the closest listed location is Eel Crag. It was named by Wainwright, for this is one of his discoveries. It is all too easy to dismiss his guides as containing little of interest for the mountaineer and scrambler. While his writing indicates that he had little enthusiasm for steep rock, he nevertheless recorded some fine lower-grade scrambles – of which this is one – that are often overlooked by scramblers.

Situation: Tower Ridge lies at the head of Coledale on the crags that form the north-east flank of Crag Hill. Although this fell is not the highest peak in the immediate area, it nevertheless dominates the range because of its location and form. Its stature becomes apparent on the walk in.

Tower Ridge provides a direct route up the north-east flank of Crag Hill from the upper reaches of Coledale to within striking distance of the summit. The ridge is formed by the rocks of Eel Crag to the north and a scree-filled hollow and Scott Crag to the south.

The ridge is easily identified, for its crest stands out proudly from the supporting fell. It is fairly broad at its base but it soon narrows to a pronounced arête and has four identifiable pinnacles.

Approach: Leave the B5922 just outside and to the west of Braithwaite and pick up the Coledale Beck path. Follow this for 3km towards the head of the dale. Keep to this track as it clears Low Force to the south of the falls. Once above the falls and the rock band that they tumble over, turn due south and traverse below and beyond the screes of Eel Crag.

You should now be able to identify Tower Ridge and can approach its base via a rising traverse line that runs south–north.

Ascent: The lower section of the ridge is quite broad and littered with boulders; ascend as you see fit. The ridge starts to narrow at the first tower, when it also starts to steepen. The tower can be ascended directly, but care should be taken with the holds as the rock can be loose. An easier approach lies to the left.

Above the tower, continue up the crest over some small rock steps until a pyramid is reached; this is avoided by traversing to the right along a scree shelf and then returning to the main crest. Above the final pyramid a grass neck connects the ridge with the mountain; the summit lies 320m to the south.

Descent: Several well-trodden paths traverse the immediate area of Crag Hill and provide alternatives for onward or descent routes. The most convenient route, and one that is quite interesting, is to descend to the east along a ridge called The Scar toward Sail (773m).

From Sail, follow the path that traverses above the hollow of Long Comb, branch off to take in Outerside (568m) over Stile End (447m), and then on to Braithwaite to pick up the road and then back to the start point.

Tower Ridge

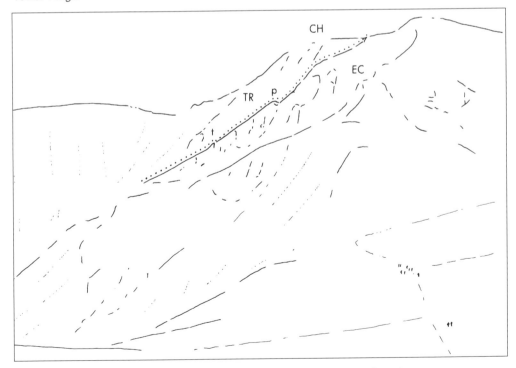

TR – Tower Ridge; CH – Crag Hill; t – tower; p – pinnacle; EC – Eel Crag

Route 42

NORTH RIDGE OF HOPEGILL HEAD

Mountain: Hopegill Head (770m)
Category: Winter and scrambling route
Grades: Scrambling – 1 (just); climbing – N/A; winter – I
Time: 5hrs
Distance: 8km
Height: 70m
Approach: GR 179 254; footpath near Y junction
Route: GR 185 227
Maps: OS 1:25,000 Outdoor Leisure sheet 4; OS 1:50,000 Landranger sheet 89

Introduction: When seen from the north, Hopegill Head takes on a fine and shapely form. This is largely due to the well-defined rock crest of its northern ridge. Under good conditions there is nothing on this route of a serious nature. Nevertheless the ridge narrows to a fine arête and there is sufficient rock combined with a fair degree of exposure to concentrate the mind.

If the remit of this book is to be followed, however, this route is best left until it has received a good covering of snow. Then the stakes are raised, crampons and an ice axe are mandatory and the ridge takes on an exhilarating air.

Situation: Hopegill Head is the highest and the central point on a broad ridge of fells that stretches from the Derwent Valley in the east to the Lorton Vale in the west. Its southern flanks consist of abrupt and rocky slopes. To the north the ground is less steep, but is breached by deep valleys and the massive rock face of Hobcarton Crag.

To the north a series of ridges radiate from Hopegill Head. The north ridge continues on to Ladyside Pike (703m)

and the western rise of Whinlatter Pass. For most of its length this ridge is broad and open, but 200m from the summit it narrows to a defined and rocky arête complete with its own breche.

Approach: From the road junction, take the path that goes south and south west over the enclosures to Littlethwaite Gill, and follow the edge of the forestry block to gain the path that runs along the broad ridge of Swinside. Follow this ridge to the summit of Ladyside Pike.

Traverse: From the summit of Ladyside Pike the rock arête becomes obvious. Simply follow the crest of the ridge to gain a pinnacle; from here the crest narrows to a well-defined edge. Next comes a pavement of rock which provides no obstacles, but a degree of exposure.

Eventually the way is barred by a breche, or notch in the rock. The scramble out of this on the far side provides the best sport on the route, but is straightforward. Off to the left the exposure is pronounced. Climb out of the breche and up the arête utilizing the alignment of the slabs that form the arête, and on to the summit.

Descent: Access is now open to the major east–west ridge of the range and several alternatives are open. It is possible to descend easily over Sand Hill (756m) to Coledale Hause to gain access to Tower Ridge (see route 40). The forestry plantations that surround Whinlatter Pass do, however, restrict descent routes to the east.

The best alternative is to head west to Whiteside (719m). Then drop down over the open hillside to the north via the head of Cold Gill, pick up the path that traverses Dodd (454m) and continue into Hope Gill to regain the road 1.25km to the south west of the start point.

*The North Ridge
of Hopegill Head*

*HH – Hopegill
Head; HC –
Hobcarton Crag;
b – breche;
LP – Ladyside
Pike*

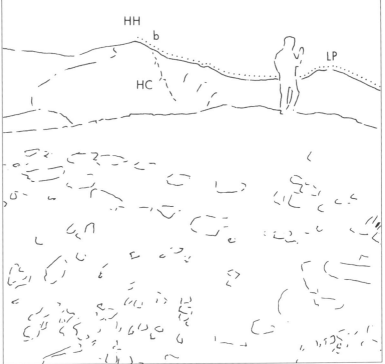

Northern Fells

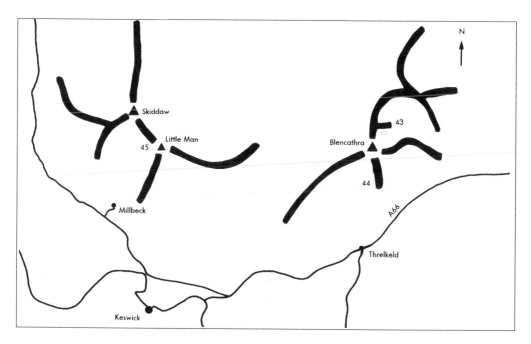

Route 43 – Sharp Edge
Route 44 – Narrow Edge of Hall's Fell Ridge
Route 45 – South-West Arête of Skiddaw Little Man

Approaches: From Keswick, the A66 or the A591. Bus service between Penrith, Keswick and Cockermouth, with drop-offs on both the A66 and A591.

Accommodation: Camping – sites off the A66 near Threlkeld and Bassenthwaite; youth hostels – Keswick and Skiddaw House; B&B and hotels – Threlkeld, Keswick and Bassenthwaite.

Tourist information: 017687 72803.

Route 43

SHARP EDGE

Mountain: Blencathra (868m)

Category: Scrambling and winter route
Grades: Scrambling – 1; climbing – N/A; winter – I
Time: 4hrs
Distance: 7km
Height: 150m
Approach: GR 340 268; lay-by on A66
Route: GR 327 283
Maps: OS 1:25,000 Outdoor Leisure sheet 5; OS 1:50,000 Landranger sheets 89 and 90

Introduction: Sharp Edge's original name was Razor Edge – both names are equally appropriate. Although only a grade 1 scramble with no technical difficulties, this is nevertheless a challenging and exhilarating route with a crux

Sharp Edge

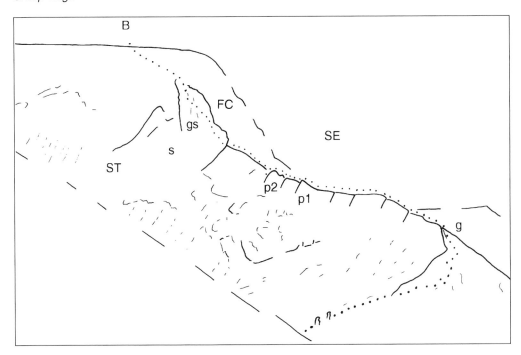

SE – Sharp Edge; B – Blencathra; ST – Scales Tarn; FC – Foule Crag; g – gully;
p1 – first pinnacle; p2 – second pinnacle; s – slabs; gs – gully system

that will make even the most experienced think twice.

Situation: A rock ridge some 400m in length, formed by the corrie of Scales Tarn to the south and Foule Crag to the north. It is connected to Blencathra's plateau by the rocks of Foule Crag which form the steep upper section of the scramble. The lower part consists of a steadily rising but narrow and continuous rock crest. There is an alternative and easier route along a path worn out of the northern flank.

Approach: The walk in is straightforward and follows a well-trodden path. From the lay-bys, follow the road east for 50m until you reach a gate complete with signpost for Scales Fell by some farm buildings. An obvious path skirts up the flank of Scales Fell around the top of Mousethwaite Comb and into the valley of the River Glendarmakin.

After just over 1km in the company of the river, a path branches off to the east alongside Scales Beck – follow this to Scales Tarn. From here the ridge dominates the corrie. A path crosses the beck and leads up the northern flank of the ridge to the edge's eastern end. This should be followed until grass gives way to rock at the start of the ridge.

Traverse: Access to the crest is provided by a well-defined angular groove that presents few difficulties; once overcome, the length of the ridge can be seen. The first part consists of broken rocks with some exposure – to the south a flank of scree, to the north grassy slopes.

The next section looks like a narrow pavement. This stretches for 30m and consists of level, solid rock about 1m in width. In dry conditions it is a pleasant stroll, but if wet or under winter conditions it will test your mettle – for in anything but dry conditions the Skiddaw Slate that makes up this ridge provides little positive grip.

Next comes a scramble down into a small notch formed by the top of a gully and a traverse around a pinnacle. Awkward in parts, the going now gets more serious as the ridge sharpens, the flanks take on a steeper angle and the exposure becomes very apparent.

After the first pinnacle comes the crux of the route, a second pinnacle blocking the crest – on its right-hand side an obvious slab, to the left a narrow ledge. Either is an option, but both have their own difficulties. The slab's outward slope and drop below can be off-putting, particularly if wet.

The rock above the slab provides little in the way of positive handholds and you must trust to your feet. On the other side the exposure is even more pronounced and the drop is almost vertical. There are sufficient holds but they are small by scrambling standards and the move is quite delicate.

Beyond this, the ridge drops to another col where Sharp Edge joins with Foule Crag and the shoulder of Blencathra. Until now the route has been along a virtually horizontal crest, but from here the character changes completely as you scramble up the steepening slabs of Foule Crag.

The best line is off to the left overlooking Scales Tarn, but if wet, the slippery rock may force you to seek the sanctuary of the gully system off to the right. After about 70m of scrambling you will emerge on to the plateau.

Descent: Blencathra's summit is about 500m to the south. An obvious path skirts the headwall above Scales Tarn and will lead you there in a matter of minutes. From here there are a number of options for descent.

One alternative is to head east over Scales Fell until you regain the original ascent route overlooking Mousethwaite Comb. The most adventurous route, however, is the direct descent from Blencathra's summit down the rocky crest of Hall's Fell Ridge (see Route 44: Narrow Edge of Hall's Fell Ridge. Both will return to you to the road.

Route 44

NARROW EDGE OF HALL'S FELL RIDGE

Mountain: Blencathra (868m)
Category: Scrambling and winter route
Grades: Scrambling – 1; climbing – N/A; winter – I
Time: 4–5hrs
Distance: 5km
Height: 268m
Approach: GR 326 258; 500m north of Threlkeld
Route: GR 326 270
Maps: OS 1:25000 Outdoor Leisure sheets 4 or 5; OS 1:50000 Landranger sheets 89 or 90

Introduction: Hall's Fell Ridge tends to be used as the descent route from Blencathra after a traverse of Sharp Edge. It is a mistake to dismiss it as such, for it has much to recommend it in its own right and deserves a better reputation. Wainwright regarded it as 'positively the best route to a summit in the district'. While it is obvious from his books that he preferred walking to scrambling, he nevertheless had an encyclopaedic knowledge of the Lakes, so his comment is worth noting.

Situation: The southern front of Blencathra rises directly above Threlkeld and the flat valley of the River Glendarmakin. While both the eastern and western flanks consist of broad grassy fell sides, the ground in between is uniformly rugged; riven by deep defiles and three steep buttresses, the latter narrow noticeably and become ridges with sharp rocky crests. The middle buttress/ridge is the finest, and this is Hall's Fell Ridge.

The lower two-thirds of Hall's Fell consist of steep grass slopes, but the final third narrows as the feature levels out. The crest is pronounced and rocky with a series of towers and pinnacles before an arête leads directly to Hall's Fell Top and the summit of Blencathra itself.

Approach: The approach is steep and unremitting. Head north down the track towards Gate Gill and on towards the open fell side beyond. A track continues up into the re-entrant formed by the gill, but ignore this and branch off north east by the weir/waterfall up the broad lower section of Hall's Fell.

There is a path, but this is not immediately apparent and it only emerges as you ascend. After 370m the ridge ahead starts to narrow noticeably and a rocky crest emerges. It is an exciting prospect.

Ascent: At first the narrowing is gradual and presents few problems. After negotiating a few small outcrops, the way is barred by a rock step. This is turned to the left by way of a traverse along a worn, horizontal band. The holds are more than adequate, but care should be taken as the exposure is noticeable.

Once the traverse is complete you will be able to ascend by a small gully to the top of a significant tower. Beyond is the 'Narrow Edge', easily dealt with in all but high winds. Beyond this is a small pinnacle which can be taken directly and this in turn is followed by an arête. The ascent of this provides the climax to the route and direct access to Blencathra's summit.

Descent: From Blencathra's summit there are several alternative descents, including reversing Sharp Edge. Perhaps the most elegant, and definitely the most direct, is to head east for 600m and pick up the path that descends down Doddick Fell Ridge.

This ridge falls just short of being

included in this book as a route in its own right. It is not quite rocky or sharp enough to be considered mountaineering, but its traverse is always stimulating and provides a fine view of the ascent route and Blencathra's south face.

The path is obvious all the way down to where the open fell changes to pasture; at this point take the east fork, cross Doddick Gill and skirt the base of Hall's Fell to intercept the outward path at the bottom of Gates Gill.

Narrow Edge of Hall's Fell Ridge

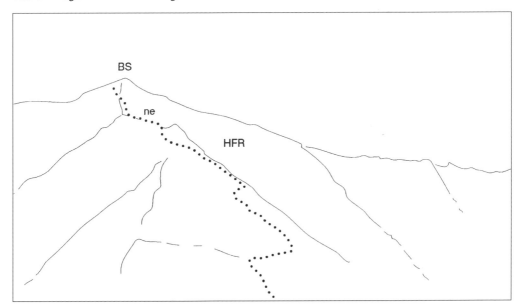

HFR – Hall's Fell Ridge; BS – Blencathra Summit; ne– narrow edge

Route 45

SOUTH-WEST ARÊTE OF SKIDDAW LITTLE MAN

Mountain: Skiddaw (931m) and Skiddaw Little Man (865m)
Category: Scrambling and winter route
Grades: Scrambling – 1; climbing – N/A; winter – I
Time: 4–5hrs
Distance: 5.2km
Height: 315m
Approach: GR 256 262; footpath west of Millbeck
Route: GR 263 276
Maps: OS 1:25,000 Outdoor Leisure sheet 4; OS 1:50,000 Landranger sheet 89 or 90

Introduction: Skiddaw stands as a distinct massif, quite separate from the other mountains of the Lake District. Its isolation is reinforced by its rock type, Skiddaw Slate, much older and more weathered than the volcanic rocks that make up the Cumbrian range. This rock, the lack of crags, and the form that the Skiddaw group takes, has little to attract the climber, scrambler or mountaineer. As a result it is too quickly dismissed as a walker's mountain with no coverage in climbing or scrambling guides.

This is a shame, for the Skiddaw range has much to offer in other aspects: it has fine views and it retains a feeling of genuine wilderness; the northern reaches of the range are more reminiscent of the Northern Pennines or even the Cairngorms than the rockier peaks of its southern neighbours. Fortunately, it has one route which is more than worthy of being called a scrambling or mountaineering route – the South-West Arête of Skiddaw Little Man.

Situation: Skiddaw Little Man is a subsidiary peak to Skiddaw's main summit, Skiddaw Man. Little Man rises directly above the hamlet of Millbeck and towers over the deep re-entrant formed by Slades Beck. The South-West Arête emerges about half way up the hillside, 180m above the confluence of Black Beck with Slade Beck.

The arête consists of a series of pinnacles that stand out from the hillside some 200m to the north east of the main bulk of Grey Crags and when seen head on appears to be a serious proposition. In reality the slope is nowhere more than 35 degrees, although it is knife-edged for much of its length. The ridge rises from a small platform above a jumble of boulders and leads directly towards the summit.

Approach: From Millbeck, pick up the narrow lane at Benny Crag. Follow this north and then north west around the wood until you gain the path that follows Slades Beck. Follow this first on the west bank and then on the east until you reach the confluence with Black Beck as it tumbles down the fell side. Ascend on the north-west bank for about 150m and then swing north over the open fell-side to the left of a scree chute. Aim for an obvious platform above the pile of boulders – this is the start of the arête.

Ascent: Above the platform is a rock rib and this can be easily negotiated by trending right. After about 10m the second platform can be gained. Above this is 120m of straightforward, but exposed and quite exciting scrambling up the knife-edge. The best sport is to be had by sticking to the crest and taking the difficulties – such as they are – head on; care should be taken with the rock, however, as it can be loose.

South-West Arête of Skiddaw Little Man

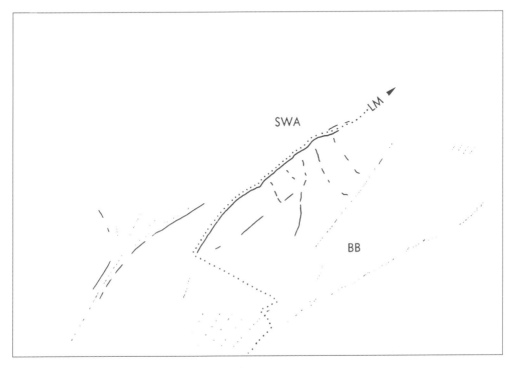

LM – Little Man; SWA – South-West Arête; BB – Black Beck

Eventually the arête loses its edge as it merges with the main mountain about 75m below the summit. This is easily reached over the summit scree.

Descent: Skiddaw's main summit is 1.5km to the north west and is reached via a very well-trodden path. It is worth retracing your steps to investigate Carl Side (746m) with its own well-known ridge, Longside Edge, and the pro-nounced pyramid of Ullock Pike (680m) with its own narrow ridge, The Edge. Unfortunately, while this route will return you to the valley, it will involve a fairly long road walk for a return to the start point.

The most direct route involves picking up the path that drops due south of Carl Side over White Stones and back to Benny Crag, Millbeck and the road.

Appendix 1
Rope and Belay Techniques

As this is a guidebook rather than a technical handbook, there is not enough space to explain properly the many varied but important techniques involved in mountaineering. There are three excellent books that go into the subject in some detail; they are *The Handbook of Climbing* by Alan Fyffe and Iain Peters (British Mountaineering Council), *Alpine Climbing* by John Barry (The Crowood Press) and *Scotland's Winter Mountains* by Martin Moran (David & Charles).

There is, however, often some confusion between the type of rope techniques used on a typical climb and the different approach usually employed on a mountaineering route. The aim of this appendix is to clarify in simple terms the methods that can be used on the variety of terrain covered in this guidebook. It does not go into sufficient detail to teach the subject; rather it is hoped that it will help someone, who may be approaching the subject for the first time, to understand the subject sufficiently to make sense of the book.

In general terms, on a climb the ground is vertical or near vertical. If a climber were to come off the rock he would fall through thin air, and if he fell for much more than 3m before hitting the ground he would probably, at the very least, be seriously injured and possibly killed. A falling climber will reach high speeds very quickly, the forces involved can be extreme and controlling them is difficult. In these circumstances,

it is essential that a fixed belay system is used.

Vertical rock, snow or ice only make up a relatively small percentage of a mountain's structure, be it an alpine peak or a British summit. Much of the terrain will have a steepish aspect, but will fall far short of being vertical; many ridges fall into this category.

Here, it is more likely that if a mountaineer slips, he would go into a slide or tumble rather than free-fall. If he cannot stop himself quickly, then matters would become more serious, but the forces involved are less extreme and easier to control. Consequently, it is feasible to move roped together and still maintain a reasonable degree of security.

FIXED BELAY SYSTEM
(Fig 1)

In essence this means that normally two people are tied to either end of a rope. One of them is always attached, or belayed to the rock and holds, or belays, the rope, feeding it out as the other climbs up. When the first climber, usually known as the leader, reaches a suitable position he attaches himself to the rock and then brings up the other, often called the second. Only one person moves at once, so if either falls off while climbing the other will hold the fall.

A fall for the second is usually of little consequence as the rope is held from above, so tightens immediately and

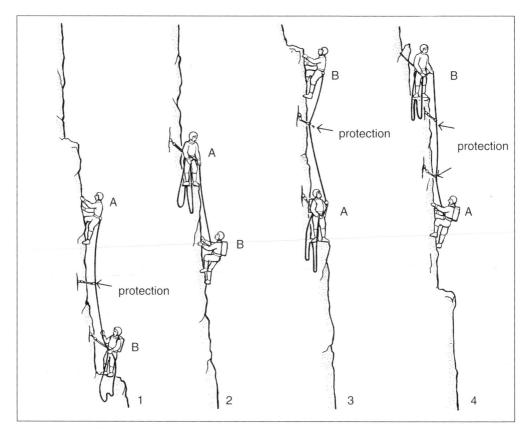

Fig 1   Fixed belay system.

stops the fall. For the leader, however, a fall can be serious as he will fall much further before the rope becomes tight. How far he falls will depend on how many running belays, often referred to as protection, he has placed.

Placing protection means placing devices, normally slings or chockstones on rock, or ice screws and deadmen on snow or ice. By using a karabiner the rope can be clipped to, but run free through the point of protection. The devices should be arranged at regular intervals, ideally every 2-3m. Each device should be secure enough to take the impact of the falling climber. If the leader falls he will then fall as far as the last piece of protection, then fall the

same distance beyond it; then, assuming the protection holds, the rope tightens and the climber comes to a stop.

This system can only work because of the in-built elasticity of modern climbing gear - ropes, protection, and harnesses. Such are the forces involved in a leader fall however, that the second's body has to absorb some of the energy as well. This means that the belayer has to be to attached to the rock and then belay the rope from his body to absorb the fall. The rope should not be belayed directly to the belay point where the impact would come directly onto the rock or ice. Without the shock being absorbed by the belayer first, there is the risk that the belay point will fail.

MOVING ROPED TOGETHER
(Figs 2-4)

The fixed belay system theoretically provides absolute security. The one problem is that it is time consuming, and this can be equally dangerous in a high mountain environment where the risk of being benighted is always present.

This is where moving roped together comes into play. Here the climbers are attached to either end of a shortened rope, ideally no more than 9m apart, and move together most of the time. If one of the mountaineers slips then he can be held by the other. The risk is that if one mountaineer takes a serious fall he can pull the other one off. This is why this method is only employed on ground where a slip will be easy to stop quickly before it gets to be more serious. Good communication is essential!

If there is a risk that a slip might be more serious then the technique can be developed. For instance, the rope can be laid in between rock pinnacles as simple running belays. If this is insufficient, slings can be placed over spikes (Fig 3). Eventually the leader will run out of slings, so a shuttle system that allows the lead to be changed or for the second to hand over the accumulated slings can be used.

On more exposed, but essentially non-technical rock, you can employ the direct belay. This allows short rock steps to be protected with one mountaineer stationary and protecting the other without resorting to the full fixed belay system (Fig 4).

To do this, the team stops and places a belay point, preferably a sling over a very reliable anchor. Using an Italian Hitch or a belay plate, the rope is attached directly to the karabiner on the

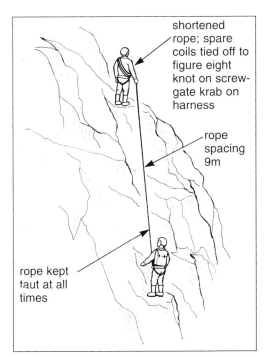

shortened rope; spare coils tied off to figure eight knot on screwgate krab on harness

rope spacing 9m

rope kept taut at all times

Fig 2   Moving roped together.

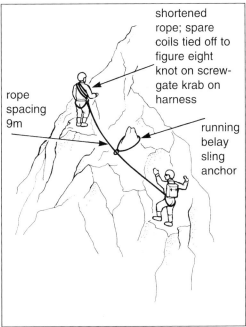

shortened rope; spare coils tied off to figure eight knot on screwgate krab on harness

rope spacing 9m

running belay sling anchor

Fig 3   Moving roped together with running belays.

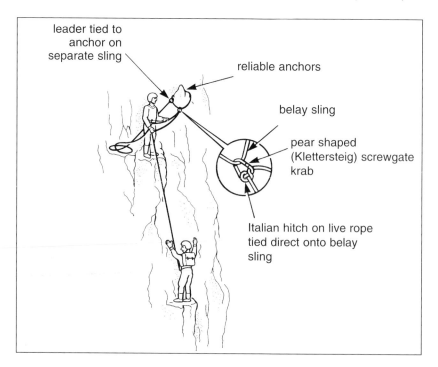

Fig 4   Direct belay.

leader tied to anchor on separate sling

reliable anchors

belay sling

pear shaped (Klettersteig) screwgate krab

Italian hitch on live rope tied direct onto belay sling

belay point and the other mountaineer is belayed directly from that. This gives a firm attachment to the rock but the belayer's body is not in the system, so he is not secure and the shock-absorbing properties of his body are not there either.

The leader can place running protection, but remember when setting up the belay that the pull will be upwards. If the leader feels he needs protection, this is perhaps the time to switch to using a full fixed belay system.

JUDGEMENT

While it is usually obvious that on a technical rock climb you will need to employ a fixed belay system, on much of the ground described in this book there can be confusion about the right techniques to employ. The answer is to be fully practised in all methods and gain the experience to make valid judgements. That can only come with time, so a healthy element of caution is recommended in the mean time.

Appendix 2
Emergency Procedure

FIRST AID CHECKLIST

Check breathing If necessary, clear the airways with a hooked finger to remove obstruction. If breathing has stopped, start mouth to mouth resuscitation.

- Check pulse If the pulse has stopped start cardiac massage. This may need to be done in conjunction with mouth to mouth resuscitation.
- Check for severe bleeding. Apply direct pressure to a bleeding wound, apply dressing and raise the limb.
- Check for broken bones. Do not move the casualty if a spinal injury is suspected. Improvise splints to immobilize the limb(s).
- Recovery position. Place casualty in the recovery position unless spinal injury is suspected.
- Monitor condition and promote recovery
- Always treat for shock, and keep the patient warm and protected from the elements.
- Continue to encourage and comfort the patient until the rescue services arrive.

ALERT EMERGENCY SERVICES

Dial 999, give your telephone number, and ask the operator for the police as they always co-ordinate mountain rescue teams. Have the following information to hand; if at all possible write it down.

- Number of casualties
- Names and descriptions of casualties
- Precise location of casualties; give a six-figure grid reference
- If the casualty is on a ridge, crag or other feature, name the route and position in relation to known features on the route so the rescuers can decide on the best approach.
- Time and nature of accident
- Extent of injuries
- Prevailing weather conditions

Remain by the phone until a police officer or member of a mountain rescue team arrives.

HELICOPTER PROCEDURE

- Secure all loose equipment before arrival of helicopter
- Identify yourself by raising your hands in a V as the helicopter approaches. Do not wave.
- Protect the injured person from rotor downdraught
- Allow the winchman to land when ready
- Do not approach the helicopter unless directed to do so by one of the crew. Beware of the danger area around the main rotor, tail rotor and the engine exhaust.

Bibliography

Allen, B., *On High Lakeland Fells* (Pic Publications, 1988)

Allen, B., *On Foot in Snowdonia* (Michael Joseph, 1993)

Ashcroft, J.B., *Britain's Highest Peaks* (David & Charles, 1993)

Ashton, S., *Scrambles in Snowdonia* (Cicerone Press, 1992)

Barry, J., *Alpine Climbing* (Crowood Press, 1988)

Bennet, R., Birkett, W., and Hyslop, A. *Winter Climbs in the Lake District* (Cicerone Press, 1979)

Butterfield, I., *The High Mountains of Britain and Ireland* (Diadem, 1986)

Campbell, M. and Newton, A., Welsh *Winter Climbs* (Cicerone Press, 1988)

Cleare, J., *Collins Guide to Mountains and Mountaineering* (Collins, 1979)

Climbers Club, *Climbers Club District Guides – Snowdonia* (Climbers Club)

Evans, R.B., *Scrambles in the Lake District* (Cicerone Press, 1982)

Evans, RB. *More Scrambles in the Lake District* (Cicerone Press 1990)

Fell and Rock Climbing Club, *Fell and Rock Climbing Club District Guides – Lake District* (Fell and Rock Climbing Club)

Fyffe, I. and Peter, I., *The Handbook of Climbing* (BMC/Pelham Books, 1990)

Moran, M., *Scotland's Winter Mountains* (David & Charles, 1988)

Thompson, G., *Classic Mountain Scrambles in England and Wales* (Mainstream, 1994)

Unsworth, W., *The Encyclopaedia of Mountaineering*(Hodder & Stoughton, 1992)

Wainwright, A., *Pictorial Guides to the Lakeland Fells, Books 1–7* (Westmorland Gazette 1955 – 66)

Index